Fashion Retail

Published in Great Britain in 2004 by Wiley-Academy,
a division of John Wiley & Sons Ltd

Copyright © 2004

John Wiley & Sons Ltd, The Atrium, Southern Gate, Chichester, West
Sussex PO19 8SQ, England Telephone (+44) 1243 779777
First published in paperback 2005

Email (for orders and customer service enquiries): cs-books@wiley.co.uk
Visit our Home Page on www.wileyeurope.com or www.wiley.com

This publication is designed to provide accurate and authoritative information in regard to the subject matter covered. It is sold on the understanding
that the Publisher is not engaged in rendering professional services. If professional advice or other expert assistance is required, the services of a
competent professional should be sought.

Other Wiley Editorial Offices

John Wiley & Sons Inc., 111 River Street, Hoboken, NJ 07030, USA

Jossey-Bass, 989 Market Street, San Francisco, CA 94103-1741, USA

Wiley-VCH Verlag GmbH, Boschstr. 12, D-69469 Weinheim, Germany

John Wiley & Sons Australia Ltd, 33 Park Road, Milton, Queensland 4064,
   Australia

John Wiley & Sons (Asia) Pte Ltd, 2 Clementi Loop #02-01, Jin Xing
   Distripark, Singapore 129809

John Wiley & Sons Canada Ltd, 22 Worcester Road, Etobicoke, Ontario,
   Canada M9W 1L1

ISBN: 0470870559

Printed and bound by Conti Tipocolor, Italy

Fashion Retail

Eleanor Curtis

Series Designer **Liz Sephton**　　Editor **Howard Watson**

contents

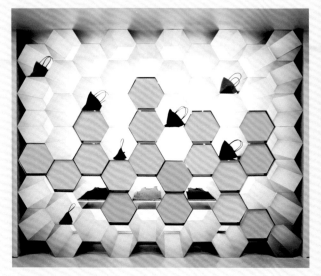

I would like to acknowledge the following for assistance with this book: Famida Rasheed, for her prompt and efficient research in response to my loaded requests; Helen Castle of Wiley, for her interest, constructive comments and helpful suggestions; also at Wiley, Mariangela Palazzi-Williams and Abigail Grater; in addition, Matteo Piazza; and all other photographers and architectural assistants who have answered my requests and provided me with all the material for the book.

Acknowledgements

The author and publisher gratefully acknowledge the following for permission to reproduce material in the book. While every effort has been made to contact copyright holders for their permission to reprint material in this book the publishers would be grateful to hear from any copyright holder who is not acknowledged here and will undertake to rectify any errors or omissions in future editions.

Photo credits

Cover: © Ed Reeve; pp 1, 5(b), 60-1, 66-9, 90-4, 96-102 & 168-173 photos: © Matteo Piazza; pp 2-3, 13(b), 152-3 & 156-63 photos: © Ramon Prat; pp 4(l), 10(tl,tr+c) & 20-33 © Office for Metropolitan Architecture; pp 4(r), 11(c+b)) 134-43 & 148-51 © Ed Reeve; pp 5(tl) & 180-1, © Curiosity Inc., photos: Theo Delhaste; pp 5(tr), 15(b), 204-5 & 208(br) courtesy Selfridges @ PA Picselect; pp 8, 13(t), 74-81, 164-5 & 198-9 © Paul Warchol; pp 8(r), 11(t), 16-7 & 34-8 © Christian Richters; pp 8(b), 9(b) & 72-3 courtesy Claudio Silvestrin, © James Morris; pp 10(b) & 40-5 © Renzo Piano Building Workshop, photos: Denancé Michel; pp 12(t) & 206 courtesy Future Systems; pp 12(b), 208(t+bl) & 209 © Future Systems, photos: Soren Aagaard; p 14(t) © Austin Reed, photo: Adrian Wilson; pp 14(b) & 196-7 © Gianfranco Ferré, photos: Paola De Pietri; p 15(t) © Jimmy Choo Ltd, photo: Jane Hanrahan; pp 46-9 © Jimmy Cohrssen/Louis Vuitton; pp 50-3 © Nacasa and Partners/Louis Vuitton; pp 54-5 © N Nakagawa/Louis Vuitton; pp 56-7 © Louis Vuitton Archives; pp 58-9 Stéphane Muratet/Louis Vuitton; pp 64-5, 70-1 © Claudio Silvestrin Archive; pp 82-9 © Dennis Gilbert/VIEW; pp 104-7, 115-7, 120-1 & 212-3 © Richard Davies; pp 112-4 © Marni, photos: Franco Rossi; pp 108-9 © Masayuki Hayashi; pp 110-1 © Yoshiko Seino; pp 118-9 © Marni, photos: Eduard Heuber; pp 122-3 © Marni, photos: Richard Davies; pp 124-7 © Chloe/SH Architects; pp 128-33 © Alexander McQueen, photos: Eric Langel; pp 144-7 © Universal Design Studio; pp 166-7 © Lydia Gould Bessler; pp 174-9 © Paul Smith/SH Architects; pp 182-5 © Curiosity Inc., photos: Shinichi Sato; pp186-91 photos: © Woo Il Kim; pp 192-5 © 6a, photos: David Grandorge; p 207 © Norbert Shoerner/Skylab Media; pp 210-1 courtesy of Harvey Nichols @ PRshots.

Preface

This book is about architecture and fashion. It is about where these two disciplines meet, initiated as an architectural commission by the fashion house, and what form this 'marriage' of design takes. Architecture and fashion relate on many different levels and the output of their relation may take many different forms. However, within the last five years it appears as though fashion has re-discovered architecture as an investment to give depth to the brand. We are seeing fashion houses, from the largest to the smallest, inviting signature architects and creating in-house teams to add value to the built environment within which they are housed.

The broad term 'fashion' is often used to refer to one and all of the many different things that we think of as being 'fashionable' be it haute couture, designer labels, garments, shoes, sunglasses or accessories. Within this book, however, we have taken fashion to refer to the fashion houses or fashion designers that are at the cutting edge of design, predominantly of clothes, shoes and bags, and who appeal to an emerging market of versatile consumers who desire luxury goods. This sophisticated level of fashion can be seen to be 'democratising luxury' as it makes itself accessible to a wider audience of mixed brand loyalty. The case studies presented here show some of the latest results of this marriage; indeed, some of the stores had not even opened during the time this book was researched. In turn, some of these stores might even be in design transition as this book is distributed. Such is the nature of fashion.

As an introduction, some ideas are raised pointing to the reasons behind the high level of architectural activity in this area, and at the beginning of each chapter, the theme is introduced and explained. The projects have been grouped according to some common thread, but it is important to note that the nature of fashion is in a constant state of change and the criteria we may use to assess fashion, and all things fashionable, also change.

Fashion and Architecture

In the last five years, the interests of fashion and architecture have started to truly converge. This has happened as fashion houses have begun to realise the advantage of creating strong architecturally designed spaces while architects have reaped the benefits of the employment and exposure that fashion retail can bring. One defining moment, in terms of press coverage, is the collaboration between Miuccia Prada and Rem Koolhaas in 2000, which brought the respective figureheads of the two design disciplines together in an internationally publicised architectural rebranding and rethinking of the Prada label. This, however, was a focus for an already turning tide. Whereas, previously, the

Introduction

relationship between architecture and fashion had often been ambivalent or even grudging – serving the other strictly in terms of function and display – it had already started to shift into an exciting dynamic, where one informs the other.

In the late 1980s, London saw the pared down high-tech of Eva Jiricna's designs for Joseph on Sloane Street and the 'shop as shrine' minimalism of David Chipperfield for Issey Miyake as clear demonstrations of a new synergy with fashion. The stripped-down architectural styles created a perfect backdrop for the black and white tailoring of the 1980s and early 1990s. Now, some 20 years later on, it's possible to see fashion and architecture in terms of what they share and how they might be benefiting from collaboration. Both are about all things new; both are about responding to history with a creative form and about making manifest cultural ideas; and both are about the discovery of new materials and technologies. In addition, fashion benefits as architecture creates a platform upon which it can be displayed, and architects are able to realise their work in physical form faster than with any other building type – often in little more than three months.

Architecture and fashion first discovered their reciprocal link with the department store. Here was the first instance where the marketplace found

Jil Sander by Gabellini Associates, London.
Michael Gabellini has been designing
minimalist and elegant stores for Jil Sander
since 1993 and has completed over 80 stores
for the brand worldwide

Prada by Herzog de Meuron, Tokyo.
The architects created the whole building
as a display window for Prada

architectural form bringing many
brands, rather than stores, under
one roof. For the first time, interior
display became the critical factor
that would encourage the sale of one particular brand over another. This was the
key to the relationship: architecture and fashion can gain from an understanding
of each other's approach to design.

Outside the department store, the possibilities for architects in fashion retail
were regarded as limited. In terms of a hierarchy of building types, retail or shop
refits were the bottom of the heap. They were the starting point for an
architectural career rather than the pinnacle. The phenomenon of signature
architects of the stature of Frank Gehry being attracted to work for fashion
houses was unknown. It was not until the late 1980s and early 1990s that there
was a discernible shift in the way that architects started to view fashion retail work.
This was prompted by a recession that hit larger architectural schemes hard, but
left an opening in retail with the steady rise in consumer spending. Perhaps the
most prominent late 1980s examples of this were Branson Coates's 'aeroplane
facade' for Jigsaw on Knightsbridge and the Katherine Hamnett store on Sloane
Street, with a fishtank prominently placed in the window. However, the idea of
architecture and fashion teaming up to inform the brand was not on the agenda
of the time, and instead these sometimes 'baroque' and flamboyant interiors (in
the case of Branson Coates) remained distinct and unique alongside the first
minimalist boutiques coming through from David Chipperfield and John Pawson.

As minimalism emerged as the dominant style in the 1990s, it nurtured new
understandings and allegiances between fashion designers and architects.
Fashion designers, whose work is predominantly clean-cut and spare, aligned
themselves with architects whose work is of that nature. For example, minimalist
design guru Pawson was invited to create the store concept for minimalist
fashion guru Calvin Klein, and clean-cut fashion designer Giorgio Armani teamed
up with the clean-cut architect Claudio Silvestrin. Other pared down
fashion/architect teams include Michael Gabellini for Jil Sander and Peter Marino
for Donna Karan. The minimalist store acts as a beautifully crafted empty shell
for the display of beautifully crafted objects. No expense is spared on materials
that are often the most luxurious of the interior palette. In some ways, this
emptiness could be said to be the perfect environment for garments and their
accessories to be viewed, admired and purchased. For all its merits, minimalism
is a style that suits most, but not all.

The New Millennium

As fashion gleaned the rewards of being associated with such named architects,
as the minimalists demonstrated, fashion houses and individual clothes
designers have, in the last five years, generated a whole new breed of store.

Giorgio Armani by Claudio Silvestrin, London.
Claudio Silvestrin has now designed over 27 stores worldwide for
Giorgio Armani, complementing the sleek lines of the garments with
his monastic-like minimalism using only the most exquisite materials

Prada by Rem Koolhaas,
SoHo, New York.

Prada by Rem Koolhaas, SoHo, New York.
This Prada store in New York, designed by
Rem Koolhaas was commissioned to the tune
of $40 million

Prada by Rem Koolhaas, SoHo, New York.
Beyond restructuring the physical reality of the
brand in three realised projects in the US, Koolhaas
and OMA have designed extensive in-store
technology projects that have generated a new
integrated service structure for Prada, and aims to
give Prada (the brand) the edge on exclusivity

They have chosen signature architects, and through the assimilation of the brand into the architecture (whether by the architects intent or by the intense relationship between architect and fashion designer), a new element of the brand has been brought to life: the store now embodies the concepts of the brand. Never before have Pritzker Prize level architects such as Herzog de Meuron, Rem Koolhaas, and Renzo Piano been associated with fashion. Now, such names are leading the shoppers into the new 'shopping temples' of our consumer culture.

It has been a very exciting time for both fashion houses and architects, as architecture finds a new forum of expression in the world of retail, and fashion designers find their styles extended into the store. Working in fashion is incredibly free and creative, according to many architects, as it allows them to design environments that play on the relationship between outside and inside, and design spaces that can respond to the transitions from season to season. In addition, designing for spaces that typically have a relatively short shelf-life gives the project a certain cutting edge – the design has to have an immediate impact to make its mark if it is only going to be around for, at best, five years.

Projects range from interior refits to entire buildings, and the budgets reflect such diversity. The buildings may be monumental in scale and are incredible in both concept and form. Fashion, it could be argued, is the new forum for exciting architecture, and its potential is enormous (which is sometimes overlooked due to its association with an often 'whimsical' industry). Fashion houses are allowing, and even encouraging, architects to explore spaces, to push boundaries, to experiment with technologies and to present an ever-responding environment within which to display their products.

An Act of Distinction

The context of these commissions is one of design overload: we are bombarded with design in our everyday lives and brand names struggle to keep afloat amongst this sea of competition. Architecture is part of distinguishing the fashion brand from so many rivals and imitators. Architecture must create the narrative that grabs the customers' attention and lures them into the world of the brand.

To take one well known brand, Prada: the label is designed to become a whole way of life, a way of being, and it is the environment within which Prada is placed that carries these messages. As Aaron Betsky points out, 'The importance of such environments was succinctly shown by the artist Andreas Gursky when he photographed Prada's familiar (to some) lime-green shoe display case without a single shoe in it. Not the product, but the scene is the point.'[1] It is interesting to note Betsky's own brackets and assumption that such a scene is already familiar to a Prada-aware audience.

Hermès by Renzo Piano, Tokyo.

Prada by Herzog de Meuron, Tokyo.
The Tokyo store by Herzog de Meuron cost Prada $87 million

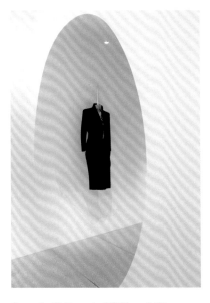

Alexander McQueen by Will Russell, Milan.
Alexander McQueen stores, now part of the Gucci group, are designed by young London architect Will Russell

Stella McCartney by Universal Design Studio, London.
Stella McCartney is one of the younger brands belonging to Gucci. This is reflected in the innovative and modern decorative approach of London-based Universal Design Studios stores

Fashion's architectural commissions are also within a context of a very real and fluctuating world economy, where survival of the fittest seems to be the underlying theme. These economic factors and the need for brand differentiation have had considerable impact on the brand's policies, and are not to be overlooked in determining the relationship between fashion and architecture.

Fashion and Figures

The fashion industry is as vulnerable to economic swings as any other industry. Recently, the war in Iraq, the SARS epidemic and the euro's strength against the dollar have all been reflected in the reported losses of the big fashion names. This slump is also in the context of a slow recession that we have endured for some years since the dot.com bubble burst in the late 1990s.

Much to our surprise, however, but in keeping with tradition perhaps, super-luxury purchases have not been so negatively affected as predicted. The extremely wealthy have continued to shop for the top of the range luxury items without too much hesitation: the latest BMW sports cars, Cartier gems, Chanel dresses and named luxury fur coats have all continued to sell well.

In reaction to this slump, however, some of the big fashion names have carried themselves over to the mass market, moving away from the exclusive, elitist customer that they traditionally sought. They have been working on attracting the 'mass-affluent' market. Prada handbags, Gucci sunglasses and Louis Vuitton suitcases have now become familiar items amongst the new middle-class buyers.

Dilution

This mass-marketing which became very evident amongst the top brands towards the end of the 1990s – a trend that reflected the 'show-off' attitudes of the prior economic period – pushed the label to reach its peak in terms of popularity. The brand name really found itself 'out there' amongst the masses. This popularity in turn knocked the edge off its 'exclusiveness', as the brand was paraded *en masse*. Luxury goods had found their mass-market and their logos were placed everywhere, whether original or fake. In essence, the brand became diluted and lost its strength.

At the same time, the bosses of the big fashion houses acquired handfuls of the luxury brands, uniting them under one holding company – in turn offering financial discipline and good commercial practice. The top end of the fashion industry is now dominated by three groups: Louis Vuitton Moet Hennessy (LVMH), Prada and Gucci.

Whilst allowing the brand to flourish in popularity, consolidation, like mass appeal, also weakened the brand and challenged the notion of 'exclusivity'. Once the brand has lost some of its credibility the fashion house seeks to re-establish value and attract custom. Making bold investments at this point in the brand's shelf-life can be seen to be very high risk, indeed immodest, but this approach seems to be the model for the way forward in order to bring the elitist, high-quality status back to the name.

Bold investments, bold design, brand differentiation

These bold investments often come in the form of financing new architecture. In the last five years 'signature' architects have been invited to bring their creative vision to literally 'house' the brand, and we are seeing some incredibly strong, sometimes beautiful and definitely innovative results. Architecture – exterior and interior – is being used to bring a certain social cachet back to the brand name.

By association with top name architects, fashion houses are adding weight to their name, conferring an almost serious, disciplined edge to a sometimes ill-

1 Aaron Betsky, 'A Matching for Living', *Logique/Visuelle: The Architecture of Louis Vuitton 2003*, Louis Vuitton (Japan 2003)

disciplined industry that is typically associated with flamboyant and dramatic personalities. The amounts being spent today on the architecture behind the brand are astounding – budgets that would have been assigned to museums and monuments a decade ago.

For example, Prada brought on board the outspoken architect Rem Koolhaas in 2001 for its store in New York at a cost of $40 million, and Herzog de Meuron, the famed Swiss architects of the Tate Modern in London, for their recent store in Tokyo to the tune of $87 million.

Before Tom Ford's acrimonious split with Gucci in 2004, he chose New York's cool Bill Solfield to give a fresh, light look for the group's YSL stores – the brand which the Gucci group are currently revamping. In addition, Alexander McQueen and Stella McCartney, also part of the Gucci group, have commissioned known architects and interior designers – Will Russell and Universal Design Studios – to strengthen their identity. However, it remains to be seen whether Pinault Printemps Redoute, Gucci's new owner, will allow the consequent level of expenditure to continue.

Even our homegrown department store – Selfridges – has boldly put itself on Birmingham's map, dominating the cityscape with its futuristic blue and silver facade. Designed by Future Systems, who have an established name in the retail world, this curvaceous building was inspired by a Paco Rabanne dress and wraps around the corner of the Bullring shopping centre like a piece of sequined fabric. The building is already being used as a city landmark in regional media.

Departures or extensions

Another trend that is emerging in response to the competition amongst fashion brands to keep one step ahead of each other, is the expansion into other market sectors. More and more fashion houses are now offering extensive homeware selections in amongst their clothing collections. For example, Nicole Farhi has been designing her own range of interiors for some time and, indeed, some of her more recent stores are incorporating display units for such items. Ralph Lauren has just recently launched a whole new chain of stores dedicated to homeware, aptly named Ralph Lauren Home. Similarly, the Armani group have established the Armani Casa stores (translated as Armani Home).

Others also offer significant spaces for eateries: Nicole Farhi's store is now more or less equally divided between fashion collections and a restaurant, and the Emporio Armani chain now offers cafés, restaurants, beauty salons and bookshops. Even the new Austin Reed flagship store in London's Regent Street has an entire floor dedicated to men's grooming. But top of the list of add-ons to stores has to be the Gianfranco Ferré Boutique and Spa in Milan. This historic palazzo is now home to all things luxurious, including a wonderful Zen-like spa.

It is interesting also to see the wonderfully designed stores for Jimmy Choo that have recently opened in New York, Milan and London, which reveal the infamous shoe designer's investment in interior architecture as a way to enhance the stores' designs and promote the brand.

Frocks, shoes, handbags, cushions, bedspreads and more, the fashion houses seem not only to be responding to increasing competition by differentiating themselves still further, but also by buying into the concept of 'lifestyle' as something that can be developed, marketed and sold. In addition, each brand now has its own 'fashion sunglasses', 'fashion perfumes', 'fashion watches' etc. that are all part of the 'lifestyle' thing. Customers are buying into the brand at all levels in an all-pervading, almost invasive way, like never before.

Store as stage

Stores are also diversifying by offering themselves as venues for art or other cultural events. Rem Koolhaas's design for Prada SoHo, New York includes a platform that emerges on command from the wavelike stairs to host cultural or

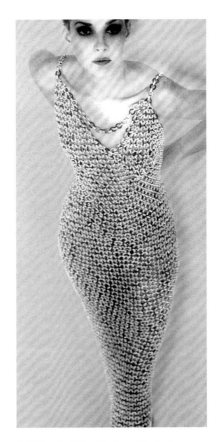

Selfridges by Future Systems, Birmingham.
The Paco Rabanne dress inspired Future Systems' concept for the new Selfridges department store in Birmingham, 2003

Selfridges by Future Systems, Birmingham.
The store now acts as the city's architectural landmark

Nicole Farhi by Gabellini Associates, New York.
As well as selling homeware and English designer Nicole Farhi's ready to wear collections for men and women, one third of the store is dedicated to Nicole's Restaurant

music events, the display steps offering themselves as an auditorium for the audience. In London, Will Russell's designs for Margaret Howell stores (not included here), in contrast to his designs for Alexander McQueen, create a gallery out of the store, blurring the division between shop and gallery, and between garments and art objects. Virgile and Stone's designs for Burberry in Milan include a variety of art pieces and installations by a wide range of artists.

Pushing the idea right to its edge has to be Selfridges' recent 'Body Craze' event at their famous Oxford Street store. Staged in early 2003, 'Body Craze' was an art exhibition, termed an 'uninhibited celebration of the human form', in which 600 naked people rode up and down on its escalators in full view of shoppers and press photographers alike. Has Selfridges set itself up as a 'retail theme park', as one critic put it, staging events to encourage shoppers? It seems that its mad methods have worked, as recent figures show an increase in sales and trading profits.

Democratising luxury: profile of the new shopper[2]

In keeping with the new extensions to the brand is a new type of luxury goods' consumer who is seen as a key to market expansion. These new consumers are 'democratising luxury', according to one economist. They are middle-market consumers aspiring to higher levels of quality and taste who are carrying luxury goods into another social strata.

As we see on the high street and at airports, people are wearing a $10 T-shirt by H&M or Gap and carrying a $500 bag by Gucci, or wearing a $300 watch by Calvin Klein and enjoying the aromas of the new Stella McCartney perfume at $50 a bottle. These new consumers show less brand loyalty, and are more selective than the consumers of traditional luxury products such as Cartier, YSL or Dior. These new consumers are also younger than their traditional counterparts and want the latest designs off the press.

Emporio Armani by Fuksas & Fuksas, Hong Kong.
The store includes a restaurant, flowershop, bookshop, café and beauty salon

2 'Every cloud has a satin lining', *The Economist*, 21 March 2003

Austin Reed, London.
The new flagship offers an entire floor dedicated to men's grooming

However, as mentioned earlier, if the goods become too popular they lose their value, and a brand name can easily become undermined if displayed incorrectly, or advertised poorly. For example, in response to the dilution of its name, Gucci has been buying back its brand licensing to ensure its logo only appears on products which meet its own standards of quality. The 'execution' of the luxury goods business is critical to its success or failure and in this case, the execution is about retailing. Today, 80 percent of Gucci's and Hermès' products, and all of Louis Vuitton's, are sold through directly owned or operated stores.

In addition, shoppers now have the option to shop from home via the designers' websites, including cut-price brand products. In order to compete with the new electronic retailing, the store needs to offer a memorable and worthwhile environment for the brand, making the experience of shopping much more desirable than simply 'point and click'.

Architecture and its social cachet

Returning to the original assumption that the association between architecture and fashion can bring added value to the fashion house, the question that needs examination is how a building really can give social cachet to the products it houses. Can the interior spaces and hanging rails really inform the customer about the brand?

The store is where the sale takes place and as with any other business model, it is in the execution of the business that you have to get the equation right. For fashion, this is the point of sale which means placing the right product in the right environment at the right time.

The surrounding built environment can inform the customer about the brand by reinforcing its identity with style. For example, fashion designers that are renowned for sleek lines and simple cuts tend to use architects who will reflect this in built form, and those better known for more flamboyant and colourful tailoring will tend to commission architects who will complement this style.

Today, in our all-consuming, all-pervading culture, when we purchase a product we are buying into the brand. The building, the logo, the advertising, the fashion model, even the shop assistants, in addition to the clothes and accessories themselves, all tie up this thing called 'image' or brand. In a sense, buying into this is like buying into a club membership. A customer will identify with a brand that reflects his or her tastes and will gravitate towards those names, reinforcing his or her self-image, just as one becomes a member of a club. One of the qualities that architecture can give to the overall image bought into by the customer, is in the all-encompassing nature of the built form: the store is more than just products and may say something about a way of doing, a way

Gianfranco Ferré Boutique, Milan.
The store offers shop and spa all in one, both bathed in absolute luxury

Jimmy Choo, London
The shoe chain is also taking note of the importance of interior architecture as its brand new store that opened in December 2003 on Bond Street shows. 'Sex in the City' has helped create a huge middle market for fashion house accessories such as Manolo Blahnik shoes and Prada handbags. In order to preserve their share of the market, specialist designers such as Jimmy Choo have to make sure that their retail outlets can compete at the highest level

of being, or a way to organise your own home. The design of a space can represent our social background, our income, our cultural values, our age, our aspirations. Architecture can put cities back on the map – as Frank Gehry did with the Guggenheim Museum in Bilbao or as Future Systems have recently done in Birmingham with the new Selfridges store. Architecture then, is able to give the brand its social cachet once again, and help the brand to become one of the most talked about names of the decade, without the risk of brand dilution.

Fashion and its benefits

What then for the architect? Apart from publicity on the fashion pages (which can be very powerful and effective for the architect), how can working in the fashion industry inform or promote the architect?

Could we ever consume a building or its interiors in the same way we consume a beautiful piece of clothing? Of course not. We can't acquire the building, the room, the staircase, the changing rooms, the display case, or the wardrobes, we can't take them to the cash desk to be wrapped in tissue paper for us to take home.

Or maybe we could. Taking this idea to its extreme – maybe by shopping in one of these stores we will also be informed about the architecture and the design, and we will be able to buy objects by the architect, or have the architect design for our own homes. Already it is not unusual to read that the shops' architect also designed the home of a fashion icon or read about the long-term loyalty between architect and fashion designer such as Gabellini and Jil Sander or Claudio Silvestrin and Giorgio Armani. Wherever it is heading, the association between fashion and architecture is yielding some positive economic and cultural results for both sides.

The case studies in this book are presented in four different chapters. The first chapter, Spectacular Houses, looks at the incredible architectural and interior projects commissioned by the larger fashion houses including Louis Vuitton, Prada and Hermès. The second chapter, Architectural Branding, takes as its theme the synergy between architect and fashion designer as emergent in the interior architecture developed for the brand worldwide. What is interesting here is how clearly the architect's style of work relates directly to the style of the brand

he is designing for. The third chapter, Custom Made, looks at commissions by fashion houses that result in a one-off store, that although very much in line with the fashion designer's brand is also led by the location of the store. Even if an architect works on several commissions for the same fashion house, the result may not be a 'branding' of the architecture.

The final chapter, New Departments, presents case studies where new and innovative architecture is being commissioned for the larger store – in this case the English department store. Although markedly different in style, content and philosophy, as well as size to the other fashion houses presented in this book, these projects demonstrate how important interiors and architecture are becoming as the new forum upon which to distinguish and present the brand within the massive department store. They also emphasise how the changing architectural and cultural landscape of cities outside London is directly linked with fashion and is not to be overlooked, despite not being the country's capital.

'Body Craze' in Selfridges, London.
Like Prada SoHo, Selfridges London now has a direct relationship with culture, encouraging an idea of the brand beyond the normal function of retail. A groundbreaking involvement with the Japan 2000 Festival was followed by this 'art exhibition' of 600 naked people riding up and down the store's escalators

Spectacular Houses

In the realm of fashion and architecture, one of the most remarkable things the public have witnessed in the last few years is the construction of a number of impressive buildings, monumental in scale, for the big fashion houses. Two of the three dominant fashion conglomerates – Louis Vuitton and Prada – are not only leaders in terms of luxury and fashion, but are also important 'patrons' to architecture, leading architects to push design to the edge in terms of how it can serve fashion. The buildings are innovative, creative and high-tech, and interestingly, the allocated budgets are equivalent in value to those spent on public museums and other important institutions 10–15 years ago.

The whole notion of commissioning new buildings to house fashion is an interesting idea that says a lot about the importance of fashion and consumerism, or consumer behaviour. In one sense, the fashion house is attempting to promote or preserve the idea of 'exclusivity', in that the goods that it sells under a particular brand name are available only to a select few, and in turn the brand name has come to signify an exclusive range of products with a certain set of standards. Indeed, commissioning a new

Spectacular Houses

building may serve to reinforce this sense of the brand and the exclusiveness of the environment within which it is housed.

At the same time, however, the fashion house needs to be 'inclusive' or open to a wider public in order to increase its sales and to push its name even further into the public realm. Architecture can enable this in its design and its association: the 'look' of the building can promote a sense of openness and invitation, whilst an association with a signature architect, or even just the discipline of architecture, can widen the scope of the fashion brand.

In addition, there is the consumer response: astonishingly enough, the night before many of these newly commissioned buildings opened, long queues would start to form down the street. Brand loyalists inconvenienced themselves to sleep overnight on the street in order to be the first to experience the new architecture. (Examples include the opening of the Roppongi store by Louis Vuitton in Japan, and the Prada store by Herzog de Meuron in Tokyo, both 2003.)

Presented in this chapter are some recent architectural designs for buildings, facades and interiors for the larger named brands. The majority of projects are in Asia, due mostly to the availability of land and the more relaxed regulations for construction.

Two of the projects are by established European architects for European brands in Tokyo and New York. Renzo Piano, the Italian architect perhaps most widely known for his design for the Pompidou Art Centre in Paris 1977 (with UK architect Richard Rogers), designed the new headquarters for Hermès in Tokyo in the form of a 'magic lantern'; a tall, thin and elegant 11-storey building housing all things 'Hermès' from retail through to exhibition space. Dutch architect Rem Koolhaas's designs for Prada in New York, though largely interior architecture, result in the most innovative commentary on shopping and brands to date. New technologies are integrated in the store in a way that transforms the ritual of shopping into something more than just the purchase, subsuming the clients into the brand they are investing in. Ironic, then, that Koolhaas made his name in the mid-1990s with his infamous text *S, M, L, XL* that entailed a critique on architecture and consumerism.

The other projects are for Louis Vuitton stores, worldwide, that are not only outstanding in their brand-inspired designs, but also in that Louis Vuitton has gathered its own in-house architectural team to realise this physical extension of the luxury brand. The Paris-based team, led by David McNulty and Eric Carlson, works on an incredible 50–100 stores per year that can entail anything from an entire building or a facade to an interior refit. The team also works with other architectural studios who are invited to supply concepts for new stores, overseen by the Louis Vuitton in-house team. A number of projects are presented here offering a range of works – from new buildings and facades in Japan and Korea to earlier ideas for interior refits in Paris and New York. Most notable are the designs for the Roppongi store in Japan, which takes on the theme of a nightclub, and the Omotesando store whose facade is shaped like a random stack of Louis Vuitton trunks. In no other project is the translation of brand icon into architectural form as apparent.

Rem Koolhaas and the
Office for Metropolitan Architecture

Prada Epicentre

SoHo, New York 2001

Rem Koolhass and his Office for Metropolitan Architecture were invited by Prada to develop three themes in fashion retail: the design of new retail concepts for the brand; the creation of three big stores in the US; and to broadly contribute to new ideas about shopping. Although criticised in some quarters, the results have certainly marked a new departure for fashion retail.

The Dutch architect Rem Koolhaas is perhaps better known for his critiques on architecture and consumerism, including *S, M, L, XL* (010 Publications, 1995) and *The Harvard Guide to Shopping* (Taschen, 2001), than for his buildings. Prada, in turn, is known for its distinct lines of high fashion and its director, Miuccia Prada, for her very strong views on art, architecture and shopping. It was of great interest to both architects and cultural theorists alike that Prada should ask the controversial critic of consumerism to come up with some new ideas for shopping, in built form.

Beyond restructuring the physical reality of the brand in three realised projects in the US, Koolhaas and OMA have designed extensive in-store technology projects that have generated a new integrated service structure for Prada and aims to give the brand the edge on exclusivity.

Instead of a traditional flagship store, Prada conceived an 'epicentre' which would offer a diversified experience of shopping. The epicentre store is divided into many zones: the clinic, an environment for personal care and service; the archive, an inventory of current and past collections; the trading floor, an accumulation of rapidly changing information, new technologies and e-commerce; the library, areas of content and knowledge of fashion; and the street, a space for multiple activities, liberated from the pressure to buy.

The New York Epicentre is a conversion of the former Guggenheim store in SoHo, an area famous for its progressive art galleries and young urbanites – a world away from Prada's other, more typical high profile site on Fifth Avenue. On entering the store, the 'wave' of stairs leads to the lower floor, connecting both levels with a vast wooden sculpture of steps. The oversized stair, made of zebra wood, is also an informal display space for shoes and mannequins. Encased in the stair is an event platform

Above and below: **Prada Epicentre New York.**
The grand staircase, or wave, is made of zebra wood and also acts as an informal display space. The adjacent translucent polycarbonate creates a dialogue between old and new as it slightly reveals the original brick wall

Above: **Prada Epicentre New York.** Site plan

Above: **Prada Epicentre New York.** The lower level can be seen through the shaft of the cylindrical glass elevator. The 12 foot diameter 'cab' contains a display of bags, so clients can shop on their way down to the lower floor

that emerges at the push of a button, turning the area into a 200-seat auditorium for cultural events organised by the Prada Foundation. This transition is at the heart of Prada and Koolhaas's vision to transform a retail space into a venue for art-happenings in New York's cool SoHo.

Large metal cages used as display units are suspended overhead on a track system like a 'hanging city'. Even the elevator is used to display bags and other accessories. A translucent, polycarbonate wall covers the existing brick of the building, lining the stairs, and creating a dialogue between old and new.

The main lounge under the wave is also where the main dressing rooms are located. Visible from display 'mattresses' covered in techno-gel, the transparency of the room may be controlled from within the dressing room itself, so a viewer may watch someone get dressed. The dressing rooms also feature other high-tech installations: 'magic mirrors' allow the customer to see themselves from both front and back at the same time, and an integrated time-delay function can even capture and replay moments. Equipped with Radio Frequency Identity antennae, the 'garment closet' is able to register merchandise brought into the room and subsequently display an inventory of icons on a touch screen. The customer can then request additional information or browse through alternate collections.

It has been reported that these technological advances are beset with functional problems, and when they are working, they are more a curiosity for tourists than an in-store aid for Prada shoppers. There are other issues, too, including negative remarks about the quality of the detailing and the unethical use of zebra wood. Perhaps this new approach to retail has been compromised too much for the sake of 'art' and 'design', and the space resembles more a museum than a store, carrying with it the semi-sterile message of 'look but don't touch'. It seems that some Prada shoppers prefer to spend their dollars at the Fifth Avenue branch while SoHo is filled with non-purchasing tourists looking at the architecture. Despite the use of the auditorium for selected art events (such as the Tribeca Film Festival 2003), the space has not been used for more radical art events as was envisioned.

The other two US epicentre stores by Rem Koolhaas and OMA are located in Los Angeles and San Francisco. A fourth epicentre for Prada, designed by Swiss architects Herzog de Meuron, opened in Tokyo in 2003.

SPECTACULAR HOUSES

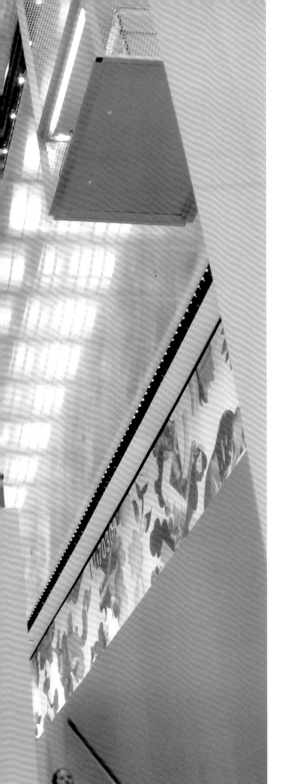

Left and above: Prada Epicentre New York.
Merchandise is displayed in movable volumes consisting of a number of aluminium-mesh cages. Suspended from the ceiling, they are configured to include hanging bars, shelving and space for mannequins and other displays. The units are mounted on motorised tracks so they can be positioned differently throughout the store

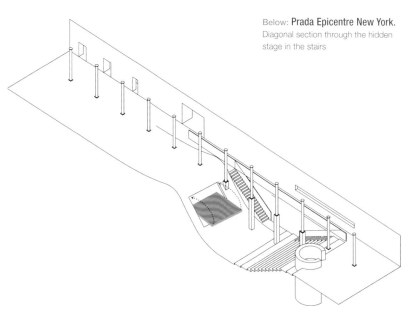

Below: Prada Epicentre New York.
Diagonal section through the hidden stage in the stairs

Above: **Prada Epicentre New York.** Suspended metal cages display Prada bags and shoes

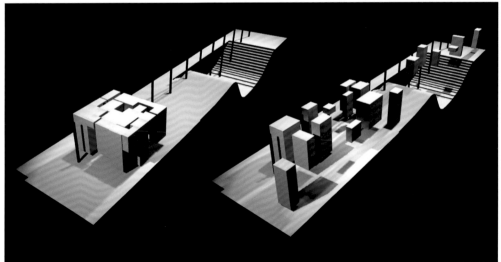

Right: **Prada Epicentre New York.** Computerised model of 'hanging city', with both open and clustered displays

Above: **Prada Epicentre New York.** Customers browse within the 'hanging city' of display units

Right: **Prada Epicentre New York.** Diagonal section through 'hanging city'

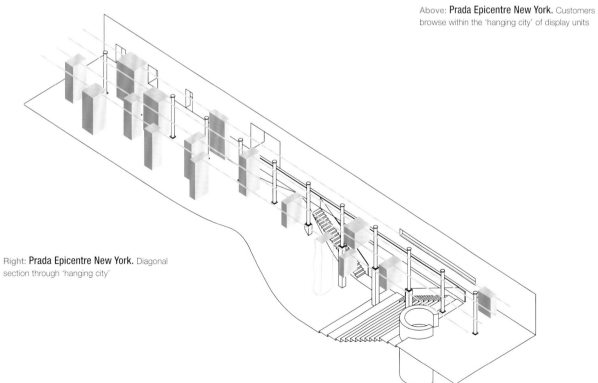

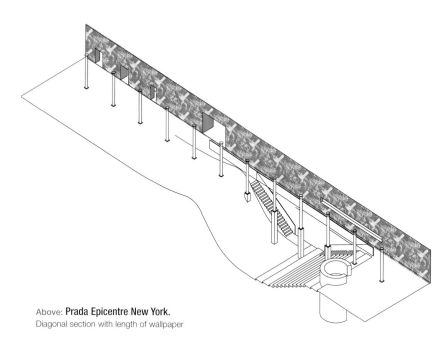

Above: **Prada Epicentre New York.**
Diagonal section with length of wallpaper

Right: **Prada Epicentre New York.**
A mural of wallpaper along the entire
length of the store offers yet another type
of environment within this retail space

Above: **Prada Epicentre New York.**
The store retains some typical SoHo
architectural details such as the raw
supporting columns on the far wall

Above: Prada Epicentre New York.
The view to the outside world is
almost unrestricted

Right: **Prada Epicentre New York.** The black and
white marble floor on the lower level makes
reference to the first Prada store in Milan;
its reflection is distorted through the curved,
mirrored ceiling of the space

Above, left and opposite: **Prada Epicentre New York.** Submerged into the display system of the store are electronic screens that show related displays of catwalks or Prada's involvement in sport or the arts, but can also be used by staff and customer as a means of communication

Purifying Gel/Face
Purifying Milk/Face
Purifying Toner/Face
Hydrating Serum/Face

Left: Prada Epicentre New York. The northern part of the lower floor holds the 'archive' zone of movable walls – a system of compact shelving that allows the size of spaces to be altered according to need

Above: Prada Epicentre New York. On the lower level, parts of the original building are revealed giving the store its very urban feel, despite the use of futuristic-type materials, lighting and layout

Herzog de Meuron

Prada Epicentre

Tokyo 2003

Following on from Prada's ambitious projects in the USA by Rem Koolhaas, most notably in New York, Prada commissioned Swiss duo Herzog de Meuron to design their Tokyo Epicentre store in the fashionable district of Aoyama. Famed for their designs for the Tate Modern in London and the recent award-winning Laban Dance Centre, also in London, Herzog de Meuron have created an extraordinary building to house Prada's fashions. They have abandoned traditional notions of the storefront in favour of a tower in which display is everything and the distinction between fashion and architecture becomes blurred.

The creation of the six-storey, five-sided glass tower enabled the architects to maximise the vertical volume of the building within its permitted gross floor area. (It is hoped that the remaining part of the lot will be a plaza, similar to the public spaces of European cities.)

The shape of the building is influenced by the possible angles of view; depending on where the onlooker is standing, the body of the building may look like either a crystal or an archaic building with a saddle roof. Its glazed surface, structured as a rhomboid-shaped grid, is clad on all five sides with a combination of convex, concave and flat panels of glass, some transparent and others etched for privacy in the changing rooms. The skin of the store looks as though it is breathing, sucking in at some angles and pouting out at others. The interiors are also characterised by disappearing surfaces or elements bubbling out of the ceilings. These different geometries offer a dazzling array of reflections which give the onlooker, either inside or outside, an ever-changing view of the Prada products, the city and themselves.

The grid design of the facade is more aesthetic: it is part of the structural engineering. Linked to the vertical cores of the building, it supports the double-height ceilings. The horizontal steel tubing helps to stiffen the overall structure and also contains private areas dedicated to the changing rooms, display units or cash desk. Multiple stairs add to the complexity of the building, which is punctuated with irregular forms intersecting the space at varying angles. 'Snorkel' shaped multimedia displays poke around the interiors like something from a sci-fi movie, offering continual footage of Prada's international collections.

All fittings, lamps and furniture are newly designed for the store and are made of either hyper-artificial materials like silicon and fibreglass, or at the other extreme, natural textures like leather, hairy pony-skin, moss or porous planks of wood.

The tower has a 'tail': a narrow wall, with oak as its main material, curls around the edge of the site, opening onto a flight of stairs that leads to the building's basement. The tail finishes with living green moss that sprouts through small squares.

Below: **Prada Tokyo.** The glazed surface, structured as a rhomboid-shaped grid, is clad on all five sides with a combination of convex, concave or flat panels of glass, some transparent and others etched for privacy in the changing rooms. The skin of the store looks as though it is breathing

Left: **Prada Tokyo.** The building abandons traditional notions of storefront in favour of a five-sided tower that acts as a big display window

Right: **Prada Tokyo.** Sections

Below and right: **Prada Tokyo.** The different geometries offer a dazzling array of reflections, which give the onlooker, either inside or outside, an ever-changing view of the Prada products, the city and themselves

PRADA

AOYAMA/H&deM/JUNE 7 2003

Above and left: Prada Tokyo. The double-height interior spaces are interrupted with horizontal steel tubes, that can contain changing rooms or display units. Some have 'snorkels' that house mutlimedia images of the building or of Prada's collections

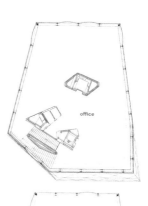

Right: **Prada Tokyo.** Plans of the store's different levels

Left: **Prada Tokyo.** Site plan showing shop's location in Aoyama area of Tokyo.

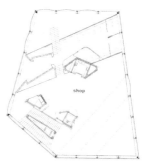

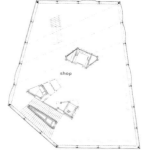

Renzo Piano Building Workshop
in collaboration with Rena Dumas
Architecture Intérieure (Paris)

Hermès

Tokyo 2001

Renzo Piano is perhaps one of today's most versatile architects. His Genoa-based office – the Renzo Piano Building Workshop – has a remarkable list of buildings and projects to its name, including landmark schemes such as the Pompidou Art Centre in Paris, Kansai Airport in Osaka, high-quality commercial buildings and a new pilgrim centre. No surprise then that Hermès invited him, with his innovative architectural vision, to design their Japanese headquarters in the Ginza district of Tokyo.

This tall, thin and elegant 11-storey building of 6,000 square metres now houses not only shopping spaces, but also floors dedicated to workshops, offices, exhibition areas and, at the top, a French-style hanging garden. With its impressive and earthquake-resistant glass-brick facade, the Maison Hermès shines like a 'magic lantern' at night.

For Piano, this project provided both aesthetic and technical challenges. How, within the architectural diversity of Tokyo, could a distinct 'landmark' building be conceived and, in turn, comply with the strict anti-seismic standards in Japan? The notion of the building lighting up Ginza, like a 'magic lantern' became the dominant theme.

The dimensions of this slim building are 45 metres long and only 11 metres wide. The facades are comprised entirely of specially designed glass blocks of 45 square centimetres, creating a continuous and luminous screen between the quiet of the inner spaces and the busy city streets. This play on interior and exterior, which changes from day to night, gives a slightly technological edge to the building, whilst retaining the concept of the traditional Japanese lantern.

A small, open square at the centre of the building connects the street to the subway station from two levels below, via a long escalator integrated into the project. A mobile sculpture by Susumu Shingu was commissioned to overlook this space from the entire height of the building, playing on the light between the facade, the city and the sky.

To cater for the possibility of earthquakes, the entire building has been designed to absorb movement according to pre-defined displacements. The backbone of the building is made up of a flexible steel structure that is articulated at strategic locations with visco-elastic dampers, from which cantilevered floors span to support the suspended glass-block facades. The integrity of the building's structure is thus guaranteed, as is that of the numerous networks that comprise the building. It is also both watertight and airtight.

Above: **Hermès Tokyo.** Detailed interior view of a corner point of the glass façade made entirely of glass bricks. The building's transparent skin allows a play between interior and exterior, and the building to change its image from day to night

Right: **Hermès Tokyo.** The entrance on the ground floor at night. The area is flooded with light and a sculpture hangs overhead emphasising the verticality of the building

Left, and right top and bottom: **Hermès Tokyo.**
Exterior views of the building, day and night. The
glass facade gives the building its slight high-tech
edge, whilst at night it reflects the architects
concept of a 'magic lantern'

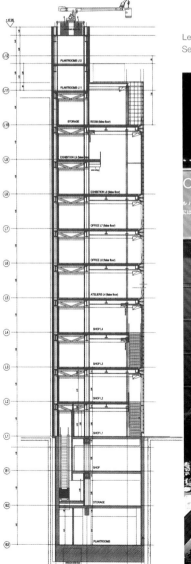

Left: **Hermès Tokyo.**
Section

Above: **Hermès Tokyo.** Interior of shop floor, flooded with natural light at the far end. A neutral pallette has been used by interior designer Rena Dumas to complement the luxurious range of clothes, bags and scarves

Below **Hermès Tokyo.**
Plan of ground floor

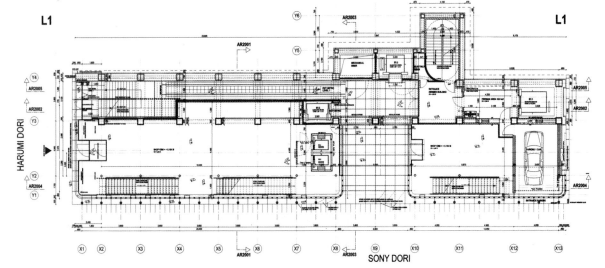

Above and right: **Hermès Tokyo.** The eleventh
floor is given over to a French-style hanging garden
while other floors are dedicated to exhibition space
or multimedia installations

Louis Vuitton architects
and associated architects

Louis Vuitton Stores

SoHo, New York 1998 (Louis Vuitton architects)
Nagoya 1999 (Jun Aoki & Associates)
Seoul 2000 (Eric Carlson/David McNulty)
Omotesando, Tokyo 2002 (Jun Aoki & Associates)
Roppongi, Tokyo 2003 (Aurelio Clementi/Jun Aoki/Eric Carlson)
Paris 2003 (Louis Vuitton architects)
Ginza, Tokyo 2004 (Jun Aoki & Associates)

The post-1997 architectural designs for the Louis Vuitton stores worldwide are finally being acknowledged as a remarkable investment and achievement in architecture. In the Aedes East gallery in Berlin, May 2003, an exhibition of the architectural work by Louis Vuitton's Paris-based in-house architectural team and associated architectural offices was titled 'Inclusive – One brand, six architects, 11 projects'; 'Inclusive' in the sense that the architecture is part of the brand's identity and is recognised as such.

Known worldwide for its luxury bags, cases and trunks with its distinctive motifs, Louis Vuitton moved into 'fashion' in 1997 with the launch of a ready-to-wear collection. This in turn stimulated the expansion of the stores with the focus on distinctive building designs related to location. With sites mostly in Asia, the group have had the opportunity to purchase or lease land parcels on which to construct entirely new buildings dedicated to the brand. In other instances, again due to the more relaxed building regulations in Asia, the team have redesigned the entire facade of a building, giving it a new skin. In Europe and North America, where exterior changes have been minimal, interior redesign has been all encompassing and exciting, often reflecting some of the facade concepts created for their Asian counterparts.

The in-house architectural team is led by Irish architect David McNulty and American architect Eric Carlson. The team's offices in Paris look like any other busy architectural studio; models, prototypes and sketches decorate the desks, tables and walls, and the environment is young and international. Other architectural studios in Paris, Verona and Tokyo are also part of the new set-up and make up the remaining five architects in the exhibition title. (20 percent of store projects are designed internally and the remaining 80 percent are managed by the Paris office using external architects.)

Louis Vuitton boasts the ownership and operation of over 300 stores worldwide, and continues to open or renovate between 50–100 new stores each year. Like the famed, iconic prints on its trunks and bags, the architecture of the stores is also reaching out to the public, reinforcing these icons in oversized 3D form, and pitching them as desirable objects in this almost surrealist world. For example, the chequerboard pattern of toile Damier has been a source of reference for a number of locations; the Sapporo store uses a giant version of a similar geometrical pattern for its display windows; Seoul uses a translucent metal mesh to cover the facade with

Above: **Louis Vuitton Roppongi.** The exterior skin is composed of over 20,000 parallel glass tubes arranged as a vast pixelised screen

reference to the texture of the fabric covering many of the LV travel chests; and taking the metaphor into the design of the building, the Louis Vuitton store in Omotesando resembles a randomly stacked set of trunks. Architecture clearly has its own strategy: to house a world-class brand and invite the public to engage with that brand. And it does so with remarkable ingenuity.

One of the more recent projects, in Roppongi, Japan, is designed by Aurelio Clementi, Jun Aoki and Eric Carlson, and strives to respond directly to the constant developments and changes in the world of fashion. Like Prada in SoHo, the store establishes the brand in a younger, hipper area than you would normally expect. Conceived with a nightclub theme, the store created such anticipation that it had a queue of potential shoppers sleeping on the street the night before the opening. The facade is composed of over 20,000 parallel glass tubes arranged as a huge pixelised screen. This two-directional sculpture produces an blurring mirage effect. The interiors are high-tech and themed around the infamous nightlife of Rappongi, with bar, lounge and fibre-optic video dancefloors overlapping with traditional retail spaces.

Other completed and ongoing projects include Japanese ventures in Kobe, designed by Philipe Barthélémy and Sylvia Grîno; Kochi, designed by Kumiko Inui; and Tokyo, by Kengo Kuma & Associates. Eric Carlson and David McNulty are responsible for outlets in Hawaii and Hong Kong, while Jun Aoki & Associates is designing a new New York store.

Presented here are some images of the recent architectural designs for the stores in Japan and South Korea, and the interior designs of two of their stores in Europe and the US.

Left and above: **Louis Vuitton Roppongi.** The 'bag-bar' is designed like a series of stacked boxes. Blacks and whites are used as base colours giving the scene very clean lines

Below: **Louis Vuitton Roppongi.** A view of the glass tube facade from within. The Louis Vuitton motif creates a texture for the white wall finishings

Left and above: Louis Vuitton Nagoya. The double skin of the building creates a vertical mist against which many displays could float. The external glass wall and the inner wall were both given the distinctive Louis Vuitton chequerboard Damier pattern, creating a hologram-type effect as a result

Right:
Louis Vuitton trunks

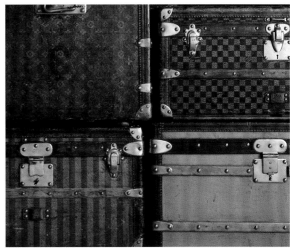

Above: **Louis Vuitton Omotesando.** The facade is transparent but monumental, allowing the onlooker a full view into the interior of the store

Left: **Louis Vuitton Omotesando.** The building is designed like a randomly stacked set of trunks

Right and far right: **Louis Vuitton Omotesando.** Close-ups of the facade. The double skin is backed by glass or steel, giving it depth

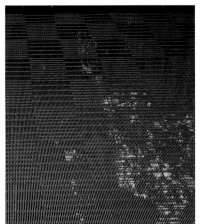

Right and left: Louis Vuitton Seoul.
The exterior is a double layered
facade composed of a Damier
patterned, mosaic tiled shell wrapped
by a stainless steel metal fabric.
Non-luxurious materials are combined
with rich textures, reminiscent of the
classic Louis Vuitton steamer trunk

Above: Louis Vuitton SoHo, New York.
View of the exterior which typifies the
architecture of the city's hip zone

Right: **Louis Vuitton SoHo, New York.** These 1998
interiors reveal the flexibility of the architectural team –
they create a rich and luxurious pallette of interior
design when structural redesign is prohibited

Below: **Louis Vuitton Paris.** View from the street

Below: **Louis Vuitton Paris.** Completed in 2003, these interiors show the evolutionary development of the Louis Vuitton stores, distinct from New York, for example, where interior architectural elements start to feature much more

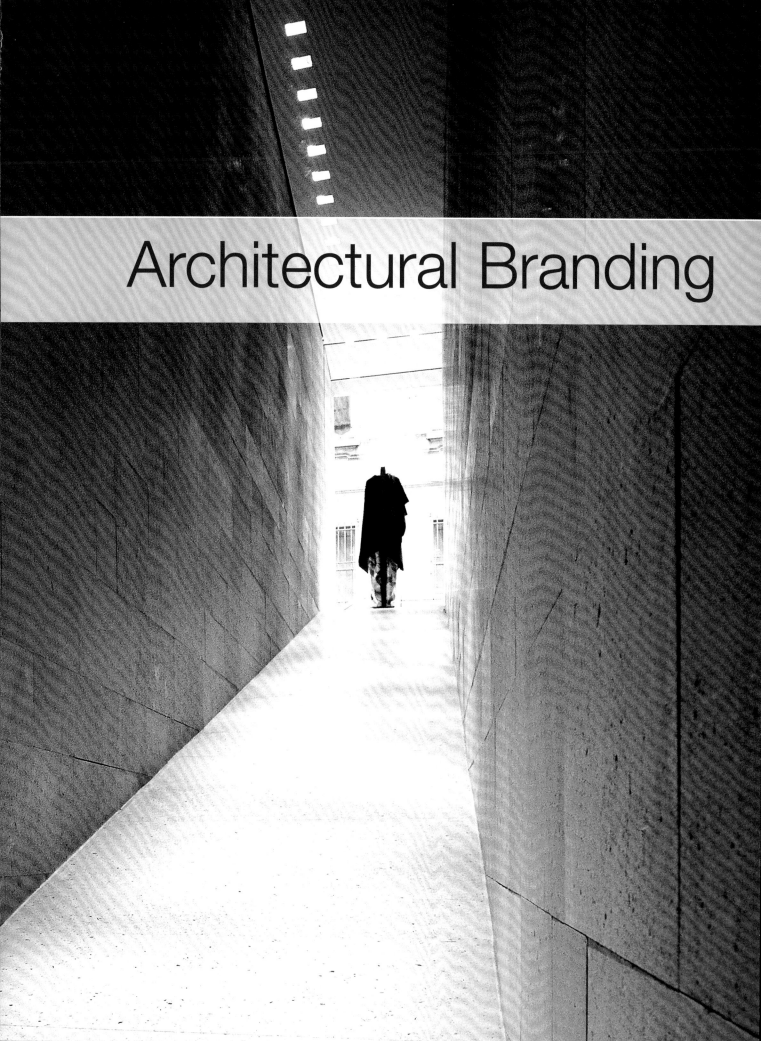

Architectural Branding

This series of project studies illustrates cases where the architect has been invited to develop an architectural concept for the brand name that may then act as a blueprint for the stores worldwide.

What emerges in this area of work are two points of interest: firstly, the synergy between the architect and the fashion designer; and secondly, the notion that an architectural concept can be relevant (or even desirable) at a global level, without being sensitive to location (just as fashion designs are aimed at a worldwide audience).

Dealing with the first issue and looking at our case studies, it is apparent that fashion designers have deliberately chosen architects whose built work can be identified with their own designs, or that they recognise that the architect's understanding of design is complementary to their own. It seems to come down to a very personal relationship between the fashion designer and the architect, and the union is one of personal tastes.

For example, Giorgio Armani, the world's leading minimalist fashion guru, chose Claudio Silvestrin, a fellow Italian and a leader in minimalist forms. Jil Sander seems to have found her architectural style with Michael Gabellini and

Architectural Branding

Gabellini Associates, whose work, although minimal, has a slightly rounded, feminine edge to it, mirroring the fine cut of Sander's clothes designs.

In all these cases, the architecture can be seen to be a direct extension of the fashion, where the styles of the garments find their home in built form. The store designs for Marni by Future Systems can also be seen to reflect the style of clothing, but pushed to the extremes of its ideas of colour and shape. The original concept by Jan Kaplicky of Future Systems was to be able to accommodate the seasonal changes of fashion in the interior architecture. There are other interesting relationships, for example, between David Chipperfield Architects and Dolce & Gabbana, where the architect has confronted the more flamboyant fashion designs with a very calm, clean, store environment with a hint of dare, allowing the garments and objects to sit harmoniously side by side. This can also be said of Will Russell's designs for Alexander McQueen stores where an almost futuristic all-white environment houses exquisite and contemporary tailoring; and Future Systems' designs for Comme des Garçons that very much reflect the ideas of the fashion house.

Another case where the architect has really looked at fashion designs in depth in order pursue a concept in architecture is Sophie Hicks Architects' design for Chloe. Sophie Hicks looked at the funky, fashionable and sexy image of Chloe and came up with an architectural concept that complemented the brand image, sometimes by playing on opposites, and carried that sensual, feminine edge into built form. Universal Design Studios concept for the Stella McCartney stores also can be said to embody much of the designs and styles of Stella in its architectural interiors.

By contrast, a project by Italian-based architects Lazzarini Pickering, for Fendi, has turned to architectural form and the use of raw materials, rather than the fashion of the brand itself, to provide the setting for luxurious items.

Perhaps these stores want to reach beyond the garment and offer something more than just shoes, bags or clothes. By pairing up with architects who complement their style, the store starts to embody the idea of the brand and reinforces the style through solid form.

The second aspect to this work is the idea that the architect can develop a store concept that can be used as a worldwide blueprint for the fashion designer. While it is completely accepted that fashion can have resonance worldwide at the same moment in time, it has not always been the case that architectural styles can be 'globalised' in the same way. Many of the cases cited above involve architectural styles that have avoided translation into local architectural languages. Rather, the original design concept, which is established as true to the fashion brand, is followed in other countries. Silvestrin's stores for Giorgio Armani, for example, are almost identical in every city. This seems to work very well in reinforcing the brand concept globally and brings a sense of harmony to the brand wherever it finds itself. (Often these architects are also asked to design the concession the brand may have in larger department stores, continuing the theme in every instance.)

As a slight variation, the work for Fendi by Lazzarini Pickering is at least site-sensitive. Although very much in keeping with the fashion brand's designs, the architectural concepts respond to the individual sites. For example, Fendi Rome is located in a historical building and thus takes on the historical theme; Fendi Paris has a very distinct staircase and so the theme centres around this architectural feature; and so on.

By highlighting two or more stores designed by the same architect in the major fashion cities of London, Paris, New York, Milan and Tokyo, the ten projects presented in this chapter give a broad insight into the way a fashion brand can find its expression in architecture.

Claudio Silvestrin Architects

Giorgio Armani

Paris, 1999
Milan 2000
São Paulo 2001
London 2003

Giorgio Armani and Claudio Silvestrin are two names that sit very well together, creating between them a harmonious reciprocity between clothing and architecture. Armani is one of the few international fashion houses that has remained a family business, and a very successful one at that. Part of its prosperity lies in its loyal commitment to a very distinct style of fashion that never seems to deviate too far. Known for sleek lines, minimalist fashions and his own token black uniform, Armani chose Claudio Silvestrin – minimalist, thoughtful, elegant, and also Italian – as the architect for his stores.

To date, Silvestrin has designed 27 Giorgio Armani stores worldwide, the first in Paris in 1999 and the most recent in Sloane Street, London in 2003. The combination of Armani's clean lines and Silvestrin's own commitment to minimalism and elegance has resulted in almost monastic-like spaces, where raw stone and beautiful cloth sit side by side. The stores are refined, simple and spatial, using exquisite materials – such as ebony, limestone and granite – to create a timeless quality, much like an art gallery. Suits and dresses hang almost solemnly in the stores, punctuating the length of the interior walls whose long lines are created through a very distinct lack of interruption by intersections and other materials.

The locations illustrated here – from the early stores of Paris and Milan through to the more recent ones of São Paulo and London – may be distinguished by their location and exterior, but typically echo each other in their interior treatment, with a shared palette of materials, details and features reinforcing the identity of the international brand.

The global reach of Armani and the extent to which Silvestrin's store designs have been rolled out worldwide is reflected in the fact that in 2003 alone, he executed stores in Dubai, Atlanta, Busan, Rome, Barcelona and London. With a new store opening imminently in Shanghai, the Silvestrin/Armani partnership remains ongoing.

Above: **Giorgio Armani Paris.** The entrance to the store characterised by a large stone vessel, marking the simplistic approach to design found throughout the store

Below: Giorgio Armani Paris. In menswear department suits are hung quietly around an uncluttered, ebony centrepiece. A standing light illuminates from behind, reflecting off the stone walls, whilst the signature square-lights sit neatly above the drawers

Right: Giorgio Armani Paris. Lighting helps create different zones in a subtle way. Turning the corner from the entrance, ebony furnishings are introduced to complement the backdrop of limestone

Above: Giorgio Armani Milan. The length of the store is accentuated by the Macassar ebony ledge, onto which shoes, bags and other accessories are carefully placed. Lighting is subtle and elegant

Right: Giorgio Armani Milan. The entrance is defined by a subtly lit pool of water, enhancing the raw French limestone in which it sits. The plain glass facade maximises the use of natural light, another feature of Silvestrin's architecture

Above and below: Giorgio Armani Milan. The use of natural materials and the lack of ornament give the space a monastic-like quality. Spaces are defined by elegant lines and forms

Above, top and bottom: **Giorgio Armani Milan.**
The stairs to the lower floor meet the ramped
corridor which starts from the store window behind
the clothed mannequin. The sparse corridor of
limestone gives the store its religious undertones,
and shows Silvestrin's minimalism at its best

Right: **Giorgio Armani Milan.** The changing rooms are also elegant in form and monastic in quality, pronouncing Silvestrin's minimalist signature

Left: Giorgio Armani São Paulo. The exterior could easily be mistaken for a contemporary church with its solid stone walls and long elegant glimpses into the store. The long but shallow steps allow for a relaxed entrance lit by Silvestrin's signature square-lights

Right: Giorgio Armani São Paulo. An exterior shot showing the solid stone walls interrupted only by lengths of glass reaching the height of the building

Below: Giorgio Armani São Paulo. Inside, the natural light offers more straight lines amongst the contemporary and minimal furnishings

Above left and right: **Giorgio Armani London.**
The Sloane Street store is the latest in a series of
flagship stores. The choice of materials, the design
of the entrance hall and staircases, the use of
natural light and the fluidity of the space are
characteristic of Silvestrin's design concept for
Giorgio Armani. The floor and the walls are clad in
St Maximin limestone, with furniture in Macassar
ebony and oxidised brass

Gabellini Associates

Jil Sander

Hamburg 1996
London 2002
New York 2002

Gabellini Associates, based in New York, have worked on many high-fashion retail projects but have perhaps become best known for their refined, minimalist and elegant designs and restorations for the Jil Sander stores worldwide. Michael Gabellini's relationship with Jil Sander goes back to 1984 when he designed the Linda Dresner store in New York, which was then the only place where Sander's designs were available. He was invited by Sander to design her first store in Paris, 1993. Since then, Gabellini Associates have designed over 80 stores for the brand worldwide, including the head office and showroom in Hamburg and the showroom in Milan, which in turn has included a variety of unique, historic restorations.

The Hamburg showroom opened in 1996 in a restored 19th-century landmark villa on the banks of Lake Alster. The building had sustained considerable damage during the Second World War and occupation by the German Finance Ministry, and so required extensive renovation and restoration, both interior and exterior. Gabellini's architectural solutions maintained the balance between old and new; plaster reliefs and woodwork complemented the bold reconfiguration of the interiors, which were filled with custom-made furnishings and fixtures; a new stairway to the lower level was added to the original grand staircase; and a terrace, formed as part of the excavations, connects the lower level dining area to the surrouding park.

The London flagship store on the corner of Burlington Gardens and Savile Row is also sited in a prominent landmark building. Formerly occupied by a bank, this early 18th-century, grand and historic residence offered the perfect space for a contemporary retail development. Its beautiful decorative details have been meticulously restored and complemented with minimalist furnishings that reflect both Gabellini and Sander's design sensibilities. (The double-height, skylit banking hall has been a popular site for London fashion extravaganzas.) The store hosts many of Gabellini's signature design elements for the Jil Sander brand: fixtures in Macassar ebony and nickel silver sitting on honed limestone flooring; floating walls that curve around existing columns; and a carefully disguised lighting concept developed to enhance both original and contemporary features. The staircase to the VIP room and showroom on the first floor features a dramatic, domed and coffered ceiling which has been highlighted with hidden light sources. A custom-made tubular fixture, extending 10 metres down from the skylight to the ground level atrium, provides a shaft of light suspended within the atrium stairwell.

The New York flagship is the first part of a bigger project that will eventually encompass the entire six floors of the building to accommodate a showroom and offices. This project also entailed the reconfiguration of the

Above: Jil Sander Hamburg. View of the very grand 19th-century landmark villa on the banks of Lake Alster. The building had sustained considerable damage during the Second World War and occupation by the German Finance Ministry, and so required extensive renovation and restoration before it re-emerged as Jil Sander's head office and showroom

Jil Sander Hamburg. Gabellini's architectural solutions maintained the balance between old and new; plaster reliefs and woodwork were completely restored to their former elegance and a new contemporary stairway (below) to the lower level was added to complement the original grand staircase (right)

limestone facade as a seamless and balanced composition that was also in keeping with neighbouring buildings. The interiors continue the historic reference with the warmth of the limestone floors and nickel silver display units alongside spare, ephemeral, and floating interior structures. The space has been altered to afford a double-height entry and triple-height backlit stair atrium. Verticality accentuating this, the west wall unfolds through the three floors as both a display wall and an ambient light source. This particular interior feature also helps navigate the client from the front of the store to the back of the space.

Above: **Jil Sander London.**
Ground floor plan

Below: **Jil Sander London.** The flagship store on
the corner of Burlington Gardens and Savile Row is
a prominent landmark building, formerly occupied
by the Royal Bank of Scotland. This early 18th
century, grand and historic residence offered the
perfect space for a contemporary retail development

Above and right: Jil Sander London. The staircase up to the VIP room and showroom on the first floor features a dramatic, domed and coffered ceiling which has been highlighted with hidden light sources. A custom-made tubular fixture, extending ten metres down from the skylight to the ground level atrium provides a shaft of light suspended within the atrium stairwell

Left: Jil Sander London. The dressing rooms occupy a ground-floor wing of the building, retaining original room height and features. Tall free-standing mirrors act as screens and offer different angles for the client

Left: **Jil Sander New York.** The interiors continue the historic reference of the facade, with the warmth of the limestone floors and nickel silver display units set alongside spare, ephemeral and floating interior structures. The space has been reconfigured to afford a double-height entry and triple-height backlit stair atrium

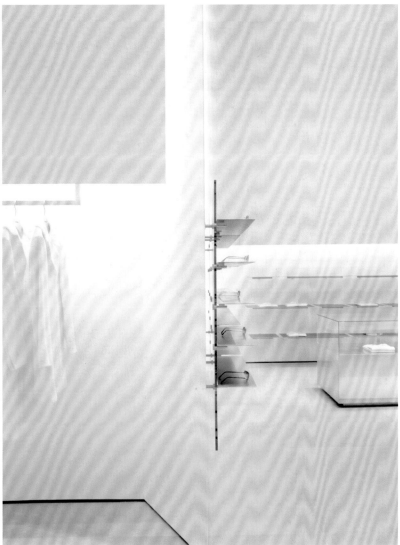

Left: **Jil Sander New York.** Minimalist and elegant, Gabellini's interiors for Jil Sander play on her own clean cut design sensibilities. Nickel silver display units hold the minimum of items in this almost transitory environment

Above: **Jil Sander New York.** The ground and first floors feature accessories, women's ready-to-wear clothes and shoes; the second floor houses men's ready-to-wear and shoes

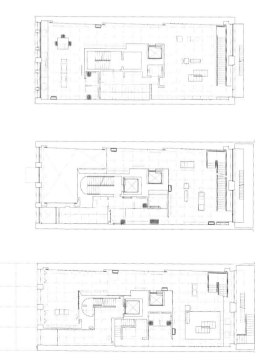

Right: **Jil Sander New York.** Floor plans

David Chipperfield

Dolce & Gabbana

London 1999
New York 2002

The internationally renowned Italian duo, Dolce & Gabbana, have carved a very distinct name for themselves in the world of fashion. Innovative, exciting and challenging are some of the adjectives that best describe their style – in terms of colour, materials, form and concept. They have retained their individualisitic identity throughout, and have escaped being swallowed up by one of the larger fashion houses.

To complement their very distinct edge on style, Dolce & Gabbana asked David Chipperfield Architects to consider the design of their worldwide identity and its realisation in shops from Osaka to Los Angeles to Paris and London. Chipperfield took as the starting point the importance of positioning the clothes as the most central elements within each store.

Rather than competing with the clothes, Chipperfield approached the idea of the store as maintaining a contrast between the extravagant, sometimes fantastical clothing with a minimalist architectural backdrop. Using natural materials with neutral colours, the architecture gives a very calm, even setting to these exciting fashion designs. Grey basalt stone extends across the entire floor area of each shop, enveloping the stairway and benches that run in ascending heights throughout the spaces, giving a monochrome surface against which the clothes stand out.

In contrast to the dark stone, the wall and ceilings are pristine white; and the laminated silk glass screens act as a canvas for special displays and also function as the boundary between sales floor and fitting room areas. The store furniture was developed by B&B Italia at the same time as the architectural concepts and it has defined a contemporary display system that is almost domestic in its simplicity. It features both wall-mounted and freestanding teak pieces, and illuminated glass cases with black stained oak accessory drawers.

Alongside the modern furniture are the signature Dolce & Gabbana furnishings: baroque chairs, oil paintings in baroque frames, zebra skins, Mediterranean plants and oversized Sicilian urns contribute to the overall sleek, but slightly exotic, interiors.

Since designing the first flagship store for Dolce & Gabbana on the Via della Spiga, Milan in 1997, which was followed two years later by the Old Bond Street store in London, Chipperfield and his office have overseen the design of 15 further outlets, including the substantial Madison Avenue store in 2002.

Above: **Dolce & Gabbana London.** View of the ground floor with the top of the staircase in view. The store is relatively minimalist and neutral in comparison to the garments it hosts

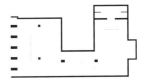

Above: **Dolce & Gabbana London.** Ground and basement plans, and section

Above: **Dolce & Gabbana London.** The new store front below
the historic facade

Above: **Dolce & Gabbana London.** Simple lines and plain surfaces are decorated with Dolce & Gabbana's exotic looking garments and flamboyant paintings

Above: **Dolce & Gabbana London.** The cold charcoal grey staircase is decorated within view with Mediterranean plants and oversized vases. Colourful garments hang gracefully at strategic points, keeping the focus on the clothes

Left: **Dolce & Gabbana New York.** Clean lines and slick features dominate the exterior view

Below: **Dolce & Gabbana New York.** View through the ground floor to the shop window with the solid charcoal cash desk to the right and the hint of the exotic with Dolce & Gabbana's signature chairs and Zebra rugs in front of the glass screen

Above: Dolce & Gabbana New York. Accessories
are simply presented on the cool contemporary
display shelves and cases, whilst dominated by
a huge urn with cactus

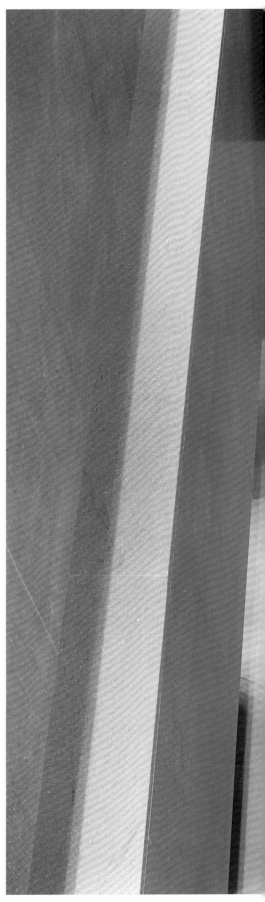

Right: Dolce & Gabbana New York. View from
the first to the ground floor. The shoes punctuate
otherwise clean and perfect lines, creating a
simple but harmonious composition of
architecture and object

Above: **Dolce & Gabbana New York.** Section
through the two floors that show length, depth and
a hint of Zebra skin

Left: Dolce & Gabbana New York. Beautiful shoes and accessories are elegantly presented on the most simple and classical forms, only slightly warmed by the Mediterranean leaves that reach out from the urn

Below: Dolce & Gabbana New York. The second floor is lit naturally with skylights and hosts the baroque mirror on the far wall, baroque chair and token cactus

Lazzarini Pickering

Fendi

London 2001
(with Househam Henderson as Executive Architects)
Paris 2001
Rome 1998–2002

Fendi, now part of the Louis Vuitton Moet Hennessy group, is perhaps best known for its luxurious leather bags and accessories, as well as sumptuous garments. The design for the Fendi stores was a collaborative effort between Rome-based architects Lazzarini Pickering and Silvia Venturini Fendi, the creative director of the company. The main thrust was to create dark and luxurious architectural interiors rather than just filling the space with products and display units. The chosen display elements – shelves, tables and suspended horizontal and vertical units – are designed as architectural objects and their size is decided in proportion to the space. For example, shelves may be as long as 10 metres, tables 7 metres, and the suspended units up to 20 metres long.

The location of each store required a slightly different architectural configuration of the basic display units and Lazzarini Pickering made use of the differences by giving a theme to each of the different stores. In London it is the facade, in Paris the staircase, and in Rome the historic building. However, the Fendi stores are highly recognisable due to their common architectural components.

In London, the distinguishing feature is the facade where display windows form the entire frontage, framed by a smooth flush white Portland stone. In the absence of a traditional shop window, the whole store becomes the display as the passer-by can view it all from the street, while the customer also becomes part of the display. This lack of division between outside and inside is augmented by the way the interior reflects details of the merchandise. The dark backdrop allows the luxury garments and accessories to be projected or emphasised. The interior materials are 'impoverished': raw sheet metal for the floor and shelves, and a layered iron-based painted render for the wall panel system and hanging volumes. The configuration of the display units is almost sculptural and at the same time informal, encouraging the client to touch or try on, and not feel overwhelmed with the formality of architectural form.

The Paris store pivots around the staircase which is a vortex of display elements that encourages clients to move from one floor to another. It is an enormous structure on which clothes, accessories, shoes and bags are placed. The use of traditional low-tech materials (as in London) has allowed for some variation; rendered surfaces are finished with an iron-based paint often used to protect metal surfaces, giving a wax finish to treated crude iron.

Lazzarini Pickering has also designed stores for Fendi in Bologna, New York, Sydney and Bangkok, with more in the pipeline.

Above: **Fendi Paris.** A long view of the store

Right: **Fendi Paris.** The design of the store pivots around the staircase

Above and left: Fendi Paris. The staircase is a vortex of display elements that encourages the client to move from one floor to another. It is an enormous display structure on which clothes, accessories, shoes and bags are placed

Above and right: **Fendi Paris.** The use of traditional low-tech materials has allowed for some variation; rendered surfaces are finished with an iron-based paint typically used to protect metal surfaces, giving a wax finish to treated crude iron

Above: **Fendi Paris.** Stand-alone furnishings are
used to distinguish other zones of the store

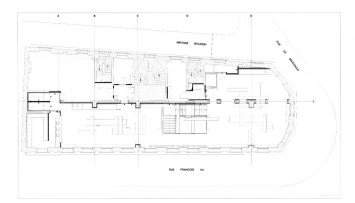

Top left: **Fendi Paris.** Ground-floor plan

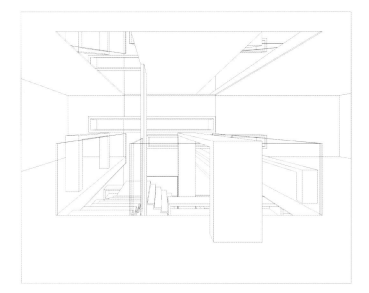

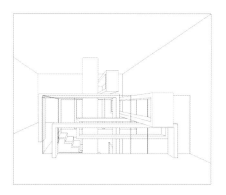

Bottom left and above: **Fendi Paris.**
Perspective views of interior

Above: **Fendi London.** The client inside the store can become part of the display. The signature architectural forms used by Lazzarini Pickering are also part of the facade

Left: **Fendi London.** In the absence of a traditional shop window the entire store becomes the display as the passer-by can view the interiors from the street

Above and top right: Fendi London. The interiors are given a dark backdrop and the materials are deliberately 'impoverished' in comparison to the luxury goods: raw sheet metal for the floor and shelves, and a layered iron-based painted render for the wall panel system and hanging volumes. The configuration of the display units is almost sculptural and at the same time informal enough not to be intimidating

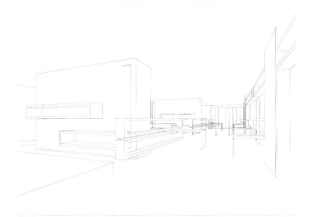

Left: **Fendi London.** Perspective of interior

Right: **Fendi London.** Floor plan

Above and right: **Fendi Rome**. The dominant theme is its historic features. The signature architectural display forms are perfectly fitting for these vaulted Italian rooms, and also sit alongside video panels that bring the old and the new face to face

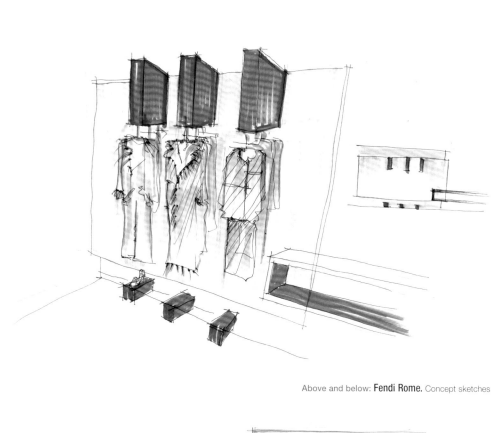

Above and below: **Fendi Rome.** Concept sketches

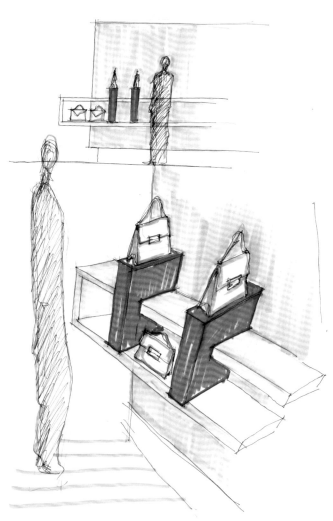

Left: **Fendi Rome.** Fendi's trademark display units intersect the space

Future Systems

COMME DES GARÇONS

New York 1998
Tokyo 1998
Paris 1999

Comme des Garçons initiated a collaboration with Future Systems in a number of different city locations. The brief was to create a new kind of space with an atmosphere of experimentation that has resulted in a powerful, uncompromising environment. The relationship between the space and the clothing is dictated by the design, its vision and the undiluted expression of the will to take risks.

The New York store, which opened in a former warehouse in 1998, is located in West Chelsea which is not an established designer retail area. Rather, it is home to many large, modern art galleries, several of which were designed by Richard Gluckman. The art crowd make it a vibrant place to be in the evenings and the clever positioning and design of the Comme des Garçons store ensure that visitors to gallery events easily seep into it. Perhaps this smooth synthesis between fashion retail and the local, cultural environment partly inspired Rem Koolhaas's vision for Prada SoHo.

Rather than create an entirely new facade, Future Systems retained the existing 19th-century fabric of the warehouse with all its old signage and external industrial fire escapes. Grafted behind the central existing brickwork, the entrance arch provides the link to the store. Juxtaposing the old with the new, the arch frames an asymmetrical, tubular entrance structure made entirely from aluminium. This link transports the individual from the streets of New York into the Comme des Garçons environment. The tube structure becomes an inbetween space, neither of the day nor the night, and not really either inside or outside. Instead, it is a fissure through an existing building into a new and challenging environment. The result is a calm yet unusual space, punctuated by a single row of marker lights. The skin of the tube has been mechanically formed and then finished by hand.

In the 1998 design for the Tokyo store, two horizontal concrete slabs of a dumb, existing building are joined with two ribbons of conically curved, inclined glass offering a simple liquid entrance at the point where they converge. The glass is covered with a layer of translucent blue dots which acts as a filter between interior and exterior. At night the movement of people within the shop creates a curiosity for the pedestrian passing the facade.

The Paris store, which opened in 1999, is the third in this series. The brief was to design a shop which was to be dedicated entirely to perfume. The historic, worn, stone facade is both protected and enhanced by a sheer skin of pale pink glass which slides gracefully in front of it.

Above and below left: Comme des Garçons New York. View of the West Chelsea store from the street. The 19th century red brick façade was retained in complete contrast to the design of the interior

Above: **Comme des Garçons New York.** The view through the tunnel into the store. Stepping into this tube from the street, with its low height and rippling texture, makes the transformation from one world to the next immediate and all encompassing

Above: **Comme des Garçons New York.**
Detail of the tunnel and the entrance door

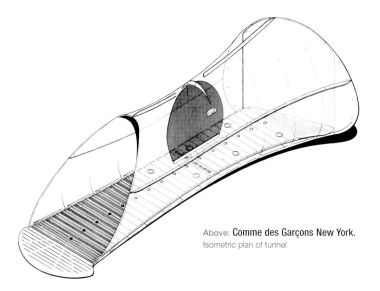

Above: **Comme des Garçons New York.**
Isometric plan of tunnel

Below: **Comme des Garçons New York.** Viewed from inside the store, the tube looks like a mouth gaping onto the real world

Left, top and bottom: **Comme des Garçons Tokyo.** Two horizontal concrete slabs of an existing building are joined with two ribbons of conically curved, inclined glass, offering a simple liquid entrance where they converge

Above, top and bottom: **Comme des Garçons Tokyo.** The glass is covered with a layer of translucent blue dots which act as a filter between interior and exterior. At night the movement of people within the shop creates a curiosity for the pedestrian passing the facade

Above: **Comme des Garçons Paris.** View of
facade of the store in Paris, dedicated to selling
perfume

Above: **Comme des Garçons Paris.**
Facade from street

Future Systems

Marni

Milan 1999
London 1999
New York 2001
Paris 2001

In the late 1990s, Future Systems, the Czech-Anglo partnership of Jan Kaplicky and Amanda Levete was asked to create a design concept for Marni stores and their concessions within department stores. Marni's colourful, eclectic fashion collections found their perfect match with Future Systems, known for its contemporary use of high-tech materials and organic forms.

Work for Marni, and indeed other creations for retail spaces (see Comme des Garçons and Selfridges profiles in this book), revolutionised ideas for store designs and stamped Future Systems' name into the fashion world in bold letters. Curvaceous and playful, Future Systems' designs are thought-provoking, questioning architecture's creative use and design of space. In a retail context such as this, it initiates innovation in the choreography of display and, specifically, how clothes hang on rails. Its work is the opposite of minimalism, deploying mostly synthetic, disposable materials and carving up the shop space with curves, arches, disks and islands.

The spirit of the stores has been generated by the clothes themselves, resulting in a composition where the store and clothes are part of one landscape. The concept was to present the clothes on a sculptural white island which sits against the brightly coloured backdrop of the rest of the shop. The original concept by Jan Kaplicky was to be able to accommodate the seasonal changes of fashion in the interior architecture by changing the coloured backdrop. The curved shape of the island is literally reflected by a mirrored stainless steel ceiling of the same shape, transforming the plan of the rectilinear shop into a space with depth and height. The background colour can be chosen to suit a particular collection and can be varied with changing seasons to give a fresh look.

Selected clothes and accessories are displayed on tall, delicate stainless steel branches or, in shops where height is limited, from stainless steel ceiling hooks. Clothes are also displayed from a stainless steel rail (which curves around the perimeter of the island), a dynamic element that changes from being a hanging rail to a flat surface for display, and then a serving counter. The clothes are hung on specially made plexiglass hangers, designed by Future Systems to be sculptural elements within the overall shop design. Unlike a traditional solution, these hang below the rail which reads as a continuous, sinuous line.

(In August 2003, the store on Sloane Street featured here was closed and Marni reopened in larger premises a few doors down. The original scheme was 'reworked' by Sybarite as described on pp 122-3. This newly imported design team are now working with Marni on an ongoing basis.)

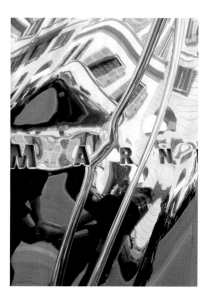

Above: **Marni Milan.** In typical Future Systems style, the door of Marni Milan plays on light, colour and reflections by using a sheet of curved steel from top to bottom

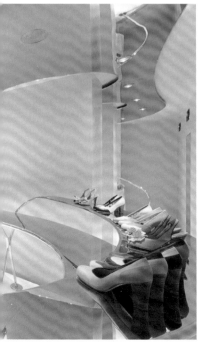

Above: Marni Milan. Detail of the clothes rail that literally wraps around the store, following the circular pathways of the walls

Left: Marni Milan. The white island reflected in the mirrored ceiling completely challenges the rectilinear plan of the shop, carving the space up with waves of clothes rails and curves of shoes. In the background are the round shop windows onto the street, shaping the view into the store

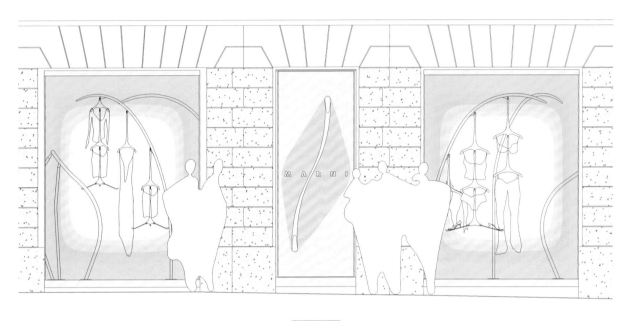

VIA S . ANDREA

Above: Marni Milan. Detail of a drawing of
the front elevation

Above: Marni Milan. Street elevation with views
into the store via the 'eye ball'

Above: **Marni London.** View of the Marni store from the street at night. (All London images are prior to the 2003 refit)

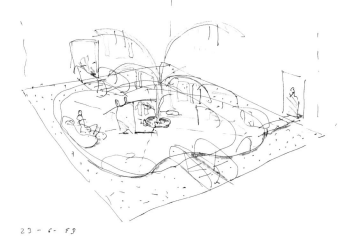

23 - 6 - 89

Left: **Marni London.** Concept sketch by founding partner of Future Systems, Jan Kaplicky

Left: **Marni London.** Long view of store, with the curves of the rails playfully carving up the blue interior, and bouncing off the mirrored ceiling

Above: **Marni London.** The clothes rail continues around the interior of the shop, wrapping its way around walls and floor

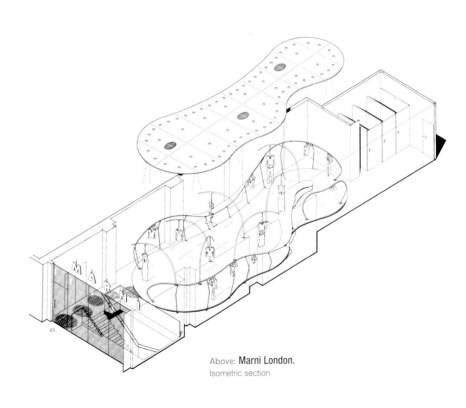

Above: **Marni London.**
Isometric section

Left: **Marni New York.** Viewed from the street, the store has had to fit into a more pre-defined space than London or Milan, with original features of the building sitting alongside Future Systems' reflective and curving design solutions

Left: **Marni New York.** A long view of the interior. With its pristine white backdrop, the store seems even more space-age than the other colourful stores of Milan or London

Left: **Marni Paris.** The store opens out with its curved white island floor and ceiling. The sinuous curves of the stainless steel display rails have been further developed to incorporate three levels of accessory shelves

Below: **Marni Paris.** The display rails sprout from the floor like trees

Above: **Marni Paris.** Reflections of rails and garments in the mirrored ceiling create height and depth to an otherwise typical store space

Above: **Marni Paris.** Detail of one of the curved
display rails with hangers also designed by
Future Systems

Sybarite

Marni

London 2003

The Sybarite refit of the new Marni store at 26 Sloane Street is testimony to just how precarious can be the ownership of an architectural concept. The look is certainly akin to that of the smaller original store further up Sloane Street, which was designed by Future Systems for Marni in 1999. The architect's hallmark features are all present – a white floor, curvilinear stainless-steel fitments and a luminous coloured backdrop. It is not, however, Future Systems' work. In this 'collaboration' between Marni fashion-designer, Consuelo Castiglioni, and architectural firm Sybarite (its partners, Torquil McIntosh and Simon Mitchell, are former members of the Future Systems office), the original conception has been thinned out and the result is colouring by numbers. The style vocabulary is all there, but the *raison d'etre* of the previous scheme has been abandoned. (It was conceived with a white-tile island floor space and mirror ceiling to provide a centre stage for constantly changing coloured backdrops, which could be adjusted in line with a season's collection.) At number 26, the red might be from within the range of the Future Systems' palette, but it lacks the sensuality and resonance of the original aqua blue. The signature Marni racks are all clustered in the middle of the expansive white resin floor, which reaches up the walls to the ceiling. The stairs are the main statement, embellished with the obligatory polished stainless-steel handrail. Certainly this new, much larger, two-storey store may know how to pull the punches, but it lacks an essential panache and conviction.

Above: Marni London. The stainless-steel trees and hangers that were a signature of Future Systems' earlier design reappear here

Below: **Marni London.** The main statement of the new two-storey Marni store is the pin-blasted stainless-steel staircase

Right: **Marni London.** In the autumn of 2003, Marni moved to a new enlarged store a few doors down Sloane Street from the original shop

Sophie Hicks Architects

Chloe

London 2002

London-based Sophie Hicks Architects was asked to develop the concept for the new Chloe stores along with the company's artistic director, Phoebe Philo. Chloe, the brand, is known for its sexy, young and luxurious designs, with a slightly provocative attitude. It gave Stella McCartney her big break when she was still fresh out of college, employing her as chief designer before she fled to Gucci and established her own brand. Sophie Hicks Architects were briefed to encapsulate and evoke the spirit of Chloe's designs in the stores.

Philo wanted the stores to be light and airy, and the first design, on London's Sloane Street, achieved this through the use of an all glass frontage, pale materials and very fragile shelving. However, the atmosphere of the store is more casual than formal. Touches of the boudoir, including gold-plated clothes rails, contrast with huge black speakers and plywood walls.

The entire design thrives on such contrasts. The display tables have salmon marble veneer tops resting on gold-plated legs, but the tops are so unusually thin and the legs are trestles, thereby managing to conjure a cheap and temporary effect from luxurious materials. The shoes are displayed on delicate shelving that faces bulky white seating. The airiness of the space is aided by the use of light-diffusing screens that merely suggest different areas, but this gives way to the dark solidity of the fitting rooms, which have low ceilings and are clothed in black satin.

Above: **Chloe London.** A concept sketch by Sophie Hicks Architects of the fitting-rooms for the flagship store

The lighting is designed as for a museum space, using spotlights to model or flood the clothes just as one would a picture or a sculpture. At night, only the mannequins and glass screens are illuminated for dramatic effect.

The door handle to the store carries Chloe's signature piece – a sculpted bronze horse in full gallop – which is to be found on every door of every store.

All in all, the new architectural concept does seem to highlight the image that Chloe wishes to portray: touches of luxury with elements of street, non-threatening style with a surprising sliver of cool.

Subsequent stores, all based on Sophie Hicks Architects' blueprint, are opening in Monaco, Seoul, Hong Kong and other destinations.

Right: **Chloe London.** Concept sketch of display areas

Below: **Chloe London.** The facade gives a clean and contemporary feel with the token bronzed horse as the door handle, Chloe's signature statement on its own strong style

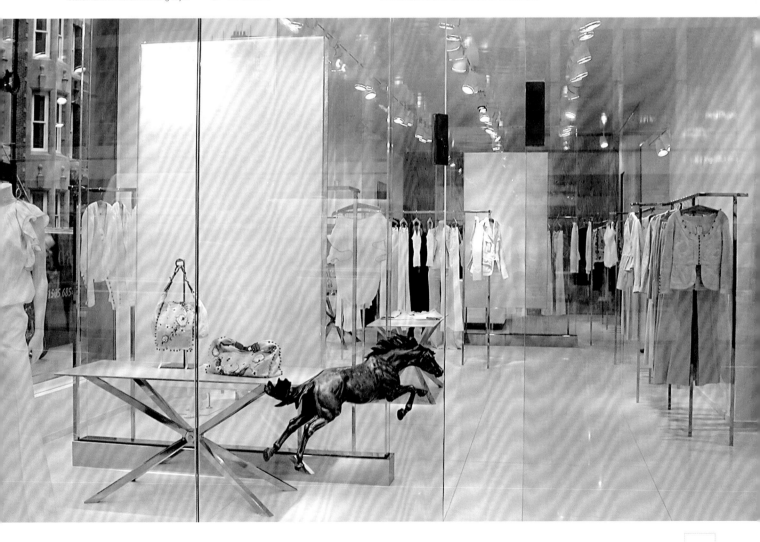

Above and left: Chloe London. The elegant and funky fashions are displayed with a backdrop of cheap plywood – the sort that would be used to board up the store in the event of a street demonstration. The salmon-coloured tabletop is so slim and delicate, it looks almost fragile resting on its gold plated trestles. Mirrors lean against walls and furniture is freestanding

Above: **Chloe London.** The fitting-rooms are
sheathed with black satin with large long mirrors
leaning against the walls, giving a very cosy,
evening feel

Will Russell

Alexander McQueen

London 2003
Milan 2003
New York 2002

Alexander McQueen, now part of the Gucci group, invited Will Russell to develop a design concept for his own brand stores that would be as distinctive as his line, and yet act as a blueprint for the outlets worldwide. Both London graduates, both London based, and both young and innovative, it seems that McQueen found his architectural match in Russell.

McQueen is just short of being known as the *enfant terrible* of fashion, with his daring, theatrical ideas that seem to find their form in exquisite tailoring; Russell, former partner of David Adjaye, is emerging from London's East End as one of the city's leading contemporary designers.

Russell looked at the project as producing an 'environment' for the brand that could be dropped in whether at flagship level or as a concession in a larger outlet. The store had to reflect the apparent contradictions in McQueen's designs – where the old meets the new, the soft with the sharp – while also being 'submissive' to the clothes themselves. McQueen was very much present in the architectural development, pushing for themes that were far from the slick modernist detail found in some retail environments, and leaning towards incorporating warm, curved and magical elements.

The New York store is in the up-and-coming Meat District of Manhattan, where numerous bars and young desiners' boutiques are mushrooming. The building is a former meat-packing warehouse that provides a wide and deep open space on a single floor. As such, the store required a focal point on entering, which was achieved with a 'mothership' – a torus-formed hanging display unit which discreetly houses the fitting rooms. The white, reflective interior takes on a space-age quality as display elements almost lose their solidity and look like fabrics as curve merges with curve. Russell conceived of the shop subtractively, as a solid block of homogenous white material from which the spaces were then carved. Light-fittings were integrated within the display elements, leaving the ceiling and wall uninterrupted from other materials. The terrazzo floor also became a continuous, resinous surface rather than being carved up by tiles.

The hanging display cabinets are modular and able to be repeated in each store environment. However, the sculpted wall and ceiling surface are more freeform and dependent on the given space.

All the stores, including London, retain these labyrinth-like qualities – even more so on the ground floor in Milan where the ceiling height is especially low (due to structural restrictions) and the store is divided into many smaller spaces. London is also split over two levels, where the staircase to the lower

Above: Alexander McQueen New York.
Accessories such as shoes and bags are beautifully placed as though objects in a gallery, carefully lit from within the display unit and reflected in mirrors opposite

Above: **Alexander McQueen New York.** Detail of the torus hanging display unit or 'mothership'. There are two entrances and a central hall of mirrors

level is the architectural focal point of the store. The staircase, an object in its own right, gives 'drama' to the store by giving a visual contact with the lower level. Milan's staircase is terrazzo and features exquisite care to detail – each step almost 'licks' the stairwall as it meets it with an upward stroke.

Being part of a larger parent holding group gave additional support to the work: Russell acknowledges that he worked closely with the Gucci Store Planning Department who have extensive knowledge of retail design for the whole of the Gucci group. Russell also designed the Alexander McQueen store in Tokyo, which opened 2001.

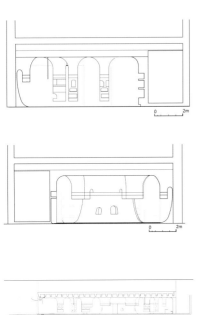

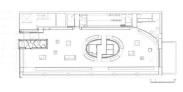

Above and below: Alexander McQueen New York. Sections and plan

Right: Alexander McQueen New York. The interior of the store is unusually deep, being a former warehouse. The space is divided into smaller units, where the unit becomes the space and almost merges into one sinuous line of white. Garments and accessories are neatly placed in the environment and decorate the view with the only instances of colour

Above: Alexander McQueen New York. The
garments offer themselves up as navigational tools
in this long, white, ethereal space

Above: Alexander McQueen New York. The smooth and continuous
terrazzo floor comes into its own, acting as a lighting board for the
hidden display unit lighting. This configuration of lights and mirrors
gives an almost futuristic feel to this gallery-type space

Above: Alexander McQueen London. View of exterior of the store on Old Bond Street. The unusual hanging display unit is apparent through the doors even from this view

Right: Alexander McQueen London. Detail of a hanging display unit that also acts as a balcony looking down to the lower floor. The column of the arch that disappears into the 'top-hat' reappears downstairs with the same curl as its frame, but in reverse

Right: Alexander McQueen London. A snapshot of the lower level over the curling balcony

Above: Alexander McQueen London. White and glowing, the store takes on an ethereal atmosphere, where accessories and garments are carefully displayed

Right: Alexander McQueen London. The garments are the only colourful element of this otherwise white and glowing store. Whole blocks are mirrored, whilst others house accessories like objects of art

Below: Alexander McQueen London.
Long section through store

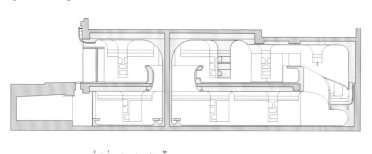

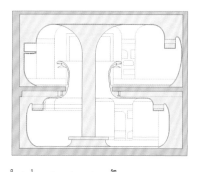

0   1   5m

Above: **Alexander McQueen London.**
Short section though store

Right, top: **Alexander McQueen London.** View down the staircase, following the curves of the store with a clothed mannequin suspended above. The terrazzo steps curl up at the edges, avoiding the use of any blunt ends in the store concept

Below, left: **Alexander McQueen London.** The ceiling of the lower level almost gets sucked into a vacuum, disappearing from view, but emanating light down the pole. These architectural details make reference to astronomical concepts, taking the store into an almost space-age type narrative

Above: **Alexander McQueen London.** Beautiful stairs and exquisite tailoring. Every line in the store follows a unique curving and undulating path

Left: **Alexander McQueen London.**
Plans of the ground (top) and lower level (bottom) floors

Above: Alexander McQueen Milan. View of the store onto Via Verri. The white arches echo through the store with almost church-like patterns

Left: Alexander McQueen Milan. View into the store from the street

Right: Alexander McQueen Milan. Display units are suspended from the curvaceous ceiling, giving a larger surface area on the terrazzo floor for reflected light to illuminate the tunnel-like space. Garments are the only elements that guide you through the white space; shoes and jewellery are exhibited like art objects in a gallery

Left: Alexander McQueen Milan. A mannequin, clad in a black suit, is suspended in this white tunnel of a curve. The architecture deliberately blurs the distinction between the straight wall and the curve

Above: Alexander McQueen Milan. View of a more customary style of display in the McQueen store, but with signature curves where the floor and the wall merge

Below: Alexander McQueen Milan. A view through the labyrinth of the store on the ground floor

Near right: Alexander McQueen Milan. White shoe shelves and a bench are gracefully incorporated into the pristine interiors, optimising the perspective of space using a mirrored wall and door

Below: Alexander McQueen Milan. Beautiful lines and gentle curves entertain the view down the stairs from the ground floor

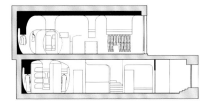

Above: Alexander McQueen Milan. Plans of ground (top) and lower level (bottom) floors

Above: Alexander McQueen Milan. Sections of ground and lower level floors

Universal Design Studio

Stella McCartney

New York 2002
London 2003

On graduating from St Martin's Art College in London, Stella McCartney walked straight into the chief designer job at Chloe and was swiftly offered her own brand within the Gucci group. The faith of Tom Ford, who also brought Alexander McQueen into the Gucci fold, was rewarded when her designs received almost unanimous approval and interest worldwide. The next step was to create her own stores along with the similarly youthful, London-based, and successful Universal Design Studio.

Common to each store is the idea of a space which will give respite to the hustle and bustle of the city – a calm and welcoming place to breathe. The first to open was the New York flagship store in 2002 in a converted warehouse on West 14th Street. The theme of an abstract landscape was developed by Universal Design Studio to create a warm and inviting atmosphere. The floor has contours and levels like a natural landscape from which clients can casually explore while the window display is set in a serene expanse of water with lily-esque display structures. The fitting rooms are hand-finished with an embroidered wall-covering designed by McCartney.

The London store, which opened a year later, is housed in a Grade II listed Georgian townhouse on Bruton Street, near Bond Street. Formerly an art gallery, the building underwent extensive refurbishments to create 6,000 square feet of retail space along with McCartney's London headquarters. The store manages to be both domestic and airy, while carrying touches of restored Georgian grandeur. The main room on the ground floor features a wall of inlaid and bejewelled designs which pick up on a nature theme that begins on the flooring. The room leads to a small but light-filled, glass-covered courtyard, and on to a backroom covered with a seemingly Georgian wallpaper, which on closer inspection reveals a rather menacing fairy tale scene designed by McCartney. Upstairs the atmosphere is redolent of the rooms of a French couturier, but all sense of the past is juxtaposed with modern elements such as contemporary furniture. The feel of the store is eclectic and very personal.

Universal Design Studio is developing a third store for McCartney in Los Angeles. However, with the departure of Tom Ford from Gucci, it remains to be seen whether the group will persevere with the level of financial clout it has put behind its young designers.

Above: **Stella McCartney New York.** View of the store from West 14th Street

Above: **Stella McCartney New York.** The window display has a water-like setting, reflecting the mannequins as if from a pool of still water

Above: Stella McCartney New York. A wide view of the interior. This vast former warehouse now offers warmth and comfort in a zone that feels far from the crowded streets. The floor contours and levels like an abstract landscape

Right: Stella McCartney New York. Bags and shoes sit comfortably with vases of green and white. Designed by Universal Design Studio, contemporary pieces of furniture complement the themed space and fashion style

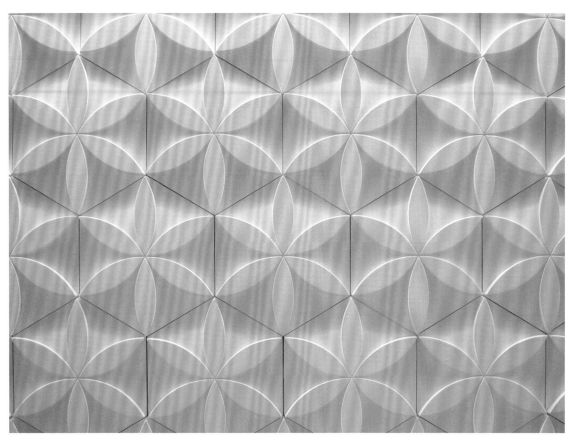

Above: **Stella McCartney New York.** Detail of tiled
wall featuring three dimensional tiles, inspired by the
hexagon

STELLA McCARTNEY, 492 WEST 14TH STREET, NEW YORK
GROUND FLOOR PLAN

Above: **Stella McCartney New York.**
Ground floor plan

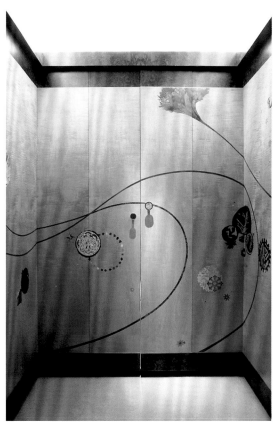

Right: **Stella McCartney New York.** Detail of
the wall covering of handpainted fabric
designed by Stella McCartney, incorporating
the theme of abstracted nature

Left: **Stella McCartney London.**
View of the flagship store and
headquarters in Bruton Street

Right and left, bottom: **Stella McCartney London.** Views of the interior. The decoration reflects the store's theme of nature with trees, branches and roots, and an almost fairy-tale like illustration designed by Stella McCartney running across the walls. Flower displays pop out of the shiny pink display unit

Above and right: Stella McCartney London.
Mannequins stand in front of the 3D tiled walls that look on to the rear patio garden. Wooden reclining deck chairs emphasise the relaxed atmosphere in this pristine white corner

Right, top and bottom: **Stella McCartney London.** Elements of the former Mayfair townhouse turned gallery are still obvious in the architecural details. The fireplace and original stucco give the store a very definite London location

Above: **Stella McCartney London.** Inside one of the changing rooms. The handprinted wallpaper is designed by Stella McCartney

Custom Made

When a fashion house requires a 'one-off' design solution for a store, often the strongest design element that emerges is formed by the architect's response to the location, which is then merged with their creative reaction to the particular fashion brand.

Each of the following projects, which are located in cities as diverse as Paris, Hong Kong, Milan, Seoul, Tokyo, London and New York, is a distinctive piece of interior architecture that reflects a bit of the city (or even the street) in which it is located. Some projects may be for a large international fashion house such as Burberry or Armani, while others are for slightly smaller but just as internationally acclaimed names such as Paul Smith and Issey Miyake.

Fuksas and Fuksas' work for Emporio Armani, daring and exciting as it is, also reflects the dare and excitement of Hong Kong's ultimate consumerist culture. This incredibly creative design uses the idea of the red ribbon, unfurling through the space, as used by Chinese gymnasts (and which is also a very strong symbol in Communist countries). The ribbon is used as the dominating architectural sculpture that shapes the navigation of this vast store.

Custom Made

In contrast, the designs by the New York-based contemporary architects Janson Goldstein, have given Emporio Armani a very different feel to their New York stores. Taking as source the neighbourhood within which it is located, the early SoHo store established a cool grey palette, using raw but smooth materials, that has carried on through to the design for the subsequent Madison Avenue store.

In the case of Virgile and Stone, who have designed the first Italian store for Burberry, both British and Italian sentiments are embodied. Burberry, the fashionable brand that carries the great British traditions of the mackintosh raincoat, the umbrella and its signature plaid check, has ingrained its Britishness in its new Milan store through the interior architecture. Virgile and Stone have sensitively brought this Britishness in line with the elegant Milanese environment, resulting in a contemporary but classy store.

Sophie Hicks Architects, who designed two stores for another British design house, Paul Smith, shows its sensitivity to location whilst retaining a sense of continuity in its approach to Paul Smith's eclectic collections. In both London and Milan, the stores are located in grand houses and the original structural features of the interior have not only been retained but emphasised, respective to their host cultures: the domestic grandeur of the London townhouse, and the heights and vaults of the Milanese palazzo.

Projects in Asia include Cho Slade's designs for the Martine Sitbon store in Seoul, that also integrates its designs in the existing architecture, but chooses to respond more to the barn than the former French villa. Curiosity's work with Gwenael Nicolas for Issey Miyake is slightly different in that the emphasis of the design is on the fashion brand rather than the location. However, references are made to each city's specific location – in Paris it is the grey brick street, in Tokyo it responds to the upmarket shopping district Aoyama.

6a and Tom Emerson introduce a completely new approach to interior design for fashion, just as the whole notion of 'shopping' is challenged by Oki-ni. The traditional transaction that takes place in the shop is no more, and instead all purchases are done by internet. What place, then, does the store have in this trade-free environment? 6a and Emerson have created a very casual store structure where both clients and store assistants can feel at ease and not at all overwhelmed by the brand.

Two other projects that only just fit into the title 'Custom Made' are those by Gabellini Associates. These projects represent more the way forward for certain types of fashion houses where the fashion goes beyond garments and accessories and enters into that all encompassing concept of 'lifestyle'. Gabellini Associates' design for the Nicole Farhi store in New York also includes a restaurant that seems as important as the store itself; and the Gianfranco Ferré store in Milan has a spa (though not designed by Gabellini Associates). Distinguished, then, by its extensions (restaurant or spa), the brand not only reinforces its identity through interior form, but also through other activities.

Massimiliano and Doriana Fuksas

Emporio Armani

Hong Kong 2002

It is a surprise to see that Giorgio Armani chose the exciting Fuksas duo to design the new Emporio Armani in Hong Kong: the Armani group is typically associated with conservative cuts and clean lines, and for the Giorgio Armani stores worldwide, Armani chose the leading minimalist architect Claudio Silvestrin for his understated sophistication. An 'emporium' is literally a warehouse, and the Armani emporium is certainly that – it is a vast store that literally sells anything from books and cosmetics to exquisite clothes and suits.

The Armani/Chater House in Hong Kong that incorporates both the clean lines of Claudio Silvestrin for the GA line and the dynamic forms of the Fuksas collaboration, carries with it a new agenda for the Armani fashion group: to appeal to a younger and more dynamic clientele than the typical Armani loyalists.

The development is strategically sited at the junction of two busy shopping streets in downtown Hong Kong. The Emporio Armani, designed by Fuksas, refuses any form of traditional architectural formalism and develops a concept of fluidity by studying the paths of people's movement through the store. The attention is less on the objects within the space than on the space itself, whether empty or decorated.

Double walls of curved glass incised with an abstract pattern move through the spaces, from internal to external, to form the backdrop for the merchandise: the effect is to render the garments apparently weightless in this almost liquid environment. The lighting systems disappear and the glass wall becomes the source of light itself. The blue-coloured epoxy resin floor, which runs throughout the store, reflects the image of the ceiling, blurring boundaries between top and bottom. The stainless steel furniture is clad in soft and translucent materials that are comfortable to use.

The transition between spaces – from the Emporio shop, through the café, the bookshop, cosmetics shop and flower shop – becomes fluid as one space disappears into another. The restaurant entertains the most thrilling detail – the red fibreglass ribbon that traces spirals in the air like the dancing ribbons of Chinese gymnasts. The red ribbon emerges, flies, and captures a wonderful sense of movement, otherwise difficult to make manifest in architecture. The intense luminosity and the colour of light in the store varies from the day to the night. The facade on Chater Road reflects the mutations of Hong Kong city with a continuously changing illuminated graphic sign.

Fuksas and Fuksas have also been invited to design the new Emporio Armani in Shanghai.

Left and right: **Emporio Armani Hong Kong.** The café on the second floor. The red fibreglass ribbon literally emerges from the floor to become a bar table, then rises and drops to create a dining space, intersects to house a DJ stand, rises to create a bar space, then turns to create a spiral tunnel that defines the main entrance. The spiral is 105 metres long, 70 centimetres wide and 8 centimetres thick

Below: **Emporio Armani Hong Kong.** The main display areas feature double walls of curved glass forming a backdrop for the merchandise

CUSTOM MADE

Above, top: **Emporio Armani Hong Kong.** The red ribbon weaves through the bar and dining area

Above, bottom: **Emporio Armani Hong Kong.** Menswear. The double glass curved wall defines the space of the store, winding its way around the garments, with black ribbons playing on this theme in the ceiling

Left: **Emporio Armani Hong Kong.** The various retail levels are connected with dramatic stainless-steel staircases with glazed treads and transparent plexiglass handrails

Left: Emporio Armani Hong Kong. In the flower shop, the vases are realised in transparent plexiglass that gives extreme lightness to the shop area and the impression that the flowers are literally floating

Right: Emporio Armani Hong Kong. The exhibition walls to the right of the bookshop are in satin plexiglass and stainless steel. The colours of the shelves alternate between red and white

Below: Emporio Armani Hong Kong. The red ribbon spirals through the entrance way

Above and top right: **Emporio Armani Hong Kong.** The cosmetics store. All furniture, designed by Fuksas and Fuksas, is made of stainless steel but clad in soft translucent plexiglass

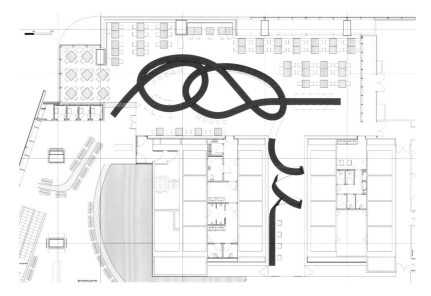

Right and far right: **Emporio Armani Hong Kong.** Café rendering and plan

Janson Goldstein

Emporio Armani

SoHo, New York 2000
Madison Avenue, New York 2003

The appointment of Janson Goldstein to design several Emporio Armani outlets can be seen as an explicit attempt to break the traditional Armani mould and reach the younger consumer. Mark Janson and Hal Goldstein have a history in retail design, having first worked on Armani projects for Naomi Leff and going on to design for DKNY, Salvatore Ferragamo and the Calvin Klein Jeans concept. They are known for large, stylish but accessible interiors that have little to do the Silvestrin-inspired minimalism of the Giorgio Armani stores.

The first store, which opened in 2000, took as its design source its unique location in SoHo, New York. Perhaps the most notable and dominating feature is its cool grey palette, which was seen to be in keeping with the 'downtown' trend of cold blacks and greys. Another reference to its SoHo location is through the materials that represent a mix of high- and low-end textures. Throughout New York's SoHo one finds the very refined 'new' in juxtaposition with the patina of the historic. In the EA space, refined materials such as Virginia Mist granite and satin stainless steel are mixed with sandblasted concrete block – an everyday material made rich by its new context.

The existing cast iron columns that occupy the centre of the space are shrouded in a sandblasted acrylic and subtly lit from within, revealing only a ghostly image of the cast iron column inside the new modern form of its acrylic enclosure.

Spatially, the store occupies one room which is defined by the store front on two sides and by the sandblasted concrete block walls on the others.

Left: **Emporio Armani SoHo, New York.** The existing cast iron columns that occupy the centre of the space are shrouded in a sandblasted acrylic and subtly lit from within, revealing only a ghostly image of the cast iron column inside the new modern form of its acrylic enclosure

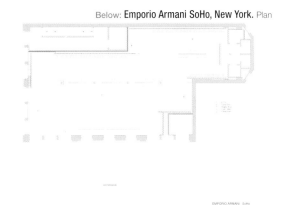

Below: **Emporio Armani SoHo, New York.** Plan

EMPORIO ARMANI SoHo

Above, top left and middle: **Emporio Armani SoHo, New York.** The store took as its design source its unique location in SoHo. Its grey palette and mix of high- and low-end materials dominate the space. Refined materials such as Virginia Mist granite and satin stainless steel are mixed with sandblasted concrete block. The only colour in the store is defined by the garments themselves

Surfaces have been designed to 'float': floors are held away from walls by a recessed trough containing neon lighting; the concrete block walls float in front of the 'container' walls that lie beyond (also incorporating a hidden light source); and the ceiling almost moves away from the adjoining walls, creating a continuous ring around the space which is utilised for hidden shades, lighting and air distribution.

The display units are made from satin stainless steel, sandblasted acrylic and cast plaster. These materials, especially where sandblasted acrylic is used in freestanding floor fixtures, provide a contrast to the Virginia Mist granite floor. Work tables are of cast plaster with stainless steel rolling drawer units that glide from below. The materials of the interior architecture are the same as those used for the fittings, limiting the entire palette of the store to a handful of textures.

The second store in Madison Avenue maintained the clean, modern aesthetic whilst introducing a new approach to the lighting designs developed with Johnson Schwinghammer. The site in Madison Avenue was originally an existing Emporio Armani store over six levels that was renovated and condensed into two levels, making the collection more accessible. The central theme in the store is the connecting stairs between the two levels that have been placed just inside the store entrance. Composed of painted steel, limestone and low-iron glass, the structure is almost suspended in the space.

The palette again is dark, as with SoHo, with dark raw plaster on the walls and ceiling, and charcoal-coloured cement fibre tiles on the floor. In contrast are backlit acrylic panels supported by a stainless-steel grid system which in turn, acts as the wall fixturing support structure.

Janson Goldstein have also designed another Emporio Armani in Los Angeles.

Second Floor - Men

1. Entry
2. Display Window
3. Elevators
4. Cash/Wrap
5. Fitting Area
6. Accessories

Ground Floor - Women

Above: Emporio Armani Madison Avenue, New York. Floor plans

Above, right, and opposite: Emporio Armani Madison Avenue, New York. The central theme in the new store is the connecting stairs between the two levels that have been placed just inside the store entrance. Composed of painted steel, limestone and low-iron glass, the structure is almost suspended in the space

Virgile and Stone with fgs
(implementation architects, Milan)

Burberry

Milan 2003

London-based Virgile and Stone were commissioned by Burberry to create a new store that would launch the British luxury brand into Italy. Burberry is perhaps best known for its 'Britishness', a theme that it has carried through into a fashionable, iconic brand, with an edge on traditional items such as the rainproof mackintosh and the umbrella. The store in Milan is the first Burberry store in Italy. The brief was to bring to life the site, a 16th-century Milanese landmark building, by encapsulating the new and progressive spirit of Burberry.

The building extends over three floors with a double-height facade that gives an immediate view, from street level, of the scale and diversity of the store. A cantilevered nickel and glass staircase links the three floors. The design approach by Virgile and Stone is 'contemporary but drawing from the heritage of the established brand' while also including contemporary art pieces from artists all over the world. Authentic British materials have been sourced but used in an innovative way; for example, the length of the building is lined with handworked English oak sitting next to high-gloss lacquered surfaces. Bespoke cabinetwork is detailed with nickel finishing, glass and lacquer.

The store is flooded with natural light and uses a natural palette of colours as the backdrop for each floor, but it is also rich in texture and tone. It is zoned into 'British scenes'. On the first floor a stylish lounge has been created, with a small bar and homely fireplace, offering a relaxed interlude from the stresses of shopping. Womenswear is more contemporary with a range of artistic details including the bound canes of Finnish artist Jakku Pernu, a large diptych by Dan Hays at the end of the room, and miniature, illuminated photographs of the catwalk placed above the hanging display units. The 'Men's Club' offers a personalised Burberry tailoring service with traditional cutting tables; suits and garments are displayed in heavy ornate oak cabinets with integrated leather straps and pockets to house accessories.

A 'Rainroom' has been especially created for the gabardine raincoat, one of Burberry's iconic garments. The British weather is celebrated with a 19-metre-long video installation piece projected on to the panelled ceiling.

There is an internal courtyard that is landscaped using traditional inlaid stone flooring and is the setting for a contemporary abstract sculpture created in collaboration with Jakku Pernu – a series of interwoven canes cut from willow, reminiscent of British country hedgerows. Other collaborations include British artists McCollin Bryan's resin cast plinths that house the new Burberry Home Collection.

Above: **Burberry Milan.** The ground floor houses bags, perfume and other accessories. The inner courtyard is accessed from the rear of the store

Right and below: **Burberry Milan.** A 'Rainroom' has been especially created for the traditional gabardine raincoat, one of Burberry's iconic garments. The British weather is celebrated with a 19-metre-long video installation piece projected on to the panelled ceiling

Burberry Milan. Womenswear on the second level has a slightly more contemporary edge to it with a range of artistic details – from the bound canes of the Finnish artist (top left), to the miniature illuminated photographs of the catwalk placed above the hanging display units (above), a seated mannequin (far left) and a large diptych by artist Dan Hays at the far end of the room (near left)

Above: Burberry Milan. The 'Men's Club' offers a personalised Burberry tailoring service with traditional cutting tables (rear of image), and shirts are traditionally laid out on individual shelves

Right: Burberry Milan. The first floor is designed with a stylish lounge in mind, akin to a typically 'British scene' with small bar and homely fireplace, offering a relaxed interlude from the stresses of shopping

Left, top, middle and bottom. **Burberry Milan.**
Accessories and perfumes are now big business for
most fashion houses, and so too is the traditional
British umbrella, housed in its own box

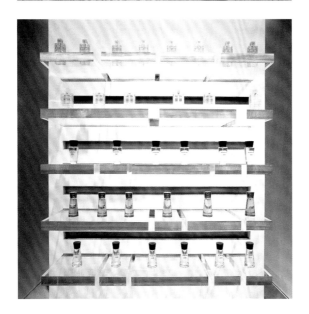

Above: **Burberry Milan**. Floor plans

Sophie Hicks Architects

Paul Smith

London 1998
Milan 2001

In contrast to many of the other projects in this chapter, Sophie Hicks Architects has deliberately reflected the location of the store in the architectural design for Paul Smith. Led by Paul Smith's almost eclectic style, the architecture for the stores is unique to each location, mirroring the eccentricity of the fashion.

Located next to Portobello Road, famous for its busy markets and its Notting Hill celebrities, Westbourne House allowed Paul Smith, who is very cautious in committing to stand-alone shops, to fulfil his wish to display his designs in a domestic house away from a hardcore retail neighbourhood. The townhouse he chose was dilapidated so the transformation into a retail outlet first required substantial rebuilding. A central atrium was created to allow more light into the house and interior walls were stripped out, but some of the names of the rooms reveal the former home's original set-up: accessories are in The Dining Room, while The Playroom is for children's wear. The clothes are displayed in furniture – dresses are hanging inside wardrobes – which evokes a domestic feel by being typical of a house of this style and period. Westbourne House has received two architectural awards and led to Sophie Hicks's appointment to design the Milan store.

Located in a site that architecturally typifies the city. Paul Smith Milan is set in the 18th-century Palazzo Gallarati Scotti which faces onto a busy street. The centrepiece of the store is a courtyard, surrounded by double-height rooms and galleries, along with smaller, more intimate spaces.

Despite the introduction of new interior features, such as illuminated dividing panels, care has been taken to emphasise the original detailing of the building and walls have been plastered using age-old, local Italian techniques. The terrazzo floor of the original palace has been kept, invigorating new designs for mosaic flooring and a very contemporary terrazzo stairway which is suspended from a hanging glass panel.

Antique furniture was sourced by the architects to match the palace's decaying beauty while plain glass has been used for the display cabinets and tabletops.

Both stores have highlighted Paul Smith's ability to transform traditional ideas with a heavy accent on the idiosyncratic and a contemporary twist. Sophie Hicks Architects will also be involved in as yet unspecified plans for New York.

Above: **Paul Smith Milan.** The double-height store gives a wonderful feeling of space and allows the vibrant pink plastered walls not to stifle the fashions. Display tables, shelves and hanging rails, in contrast, create clean and simple lines

Right: **Paul Smith Milan.** The old and the new sit side by side in this room full of colour and bathed in natural light. Ties are amusingly hung on the oversized flower, reached from the glass mezzanine level that looks down from above

Above: **Paul Smith Milan.** The original architectural features of the palazzo were retained as seen in the corridor of shelves. Paul Smith's colourful designs sit comfortably in this all-plaster, pink environment

Right: **Paul Smith Milan.** Interior view of main room, with original arched architectural features and the use of antique furniture in the foreground

Left: Paul Smith London. Exterior view of Westbourne House, a grand townhouse in the heart of Notting Hill

Below: Paul Smith London. Menswear on the ground floor where the clothes are hung in wardrobes and chandeliers hang from the ceiling, retaining the old feel of the house

Below: **Paul Smith London.** The accessories
are displayed in a traditional cabinet with a
heavy wrought-iron chandelier hanging above.
Walls throughout the house are adorned with
pictures in all shapes and sizes

Right: Paul Smith London. The glass staircase injects a very contemporary edge to the centre of this grand townhouse, flooding the house with natural light from above

Below: Paul Smith London. Detail of women's jewellery display case, with fitting chairs and lamps

Curiosity with lighting designed by
Gwenael Nicolas

Issey Miyake

Pleats Please, Paris 1999
Pleats Please, Tokyo 2000

Issey Miyake's distinctive fashion designs require a very distinctive environment within which to be displayed. Miyake's range for Pleats Please places emphasis on the most often 'crinkled' texture of the garment, as well as his famous one-seam cut. Pleats Please stores are throughout the world, and in most instances Miyake chooses different architects for each store. In this example, he commissioned Tokyo-based architects Curiosity to design both his second store in Paris on Rue des Rosiers and the store in the distinguished shopping district of Aoyama in Tokyo.

The second Pleats Please in Paris (the other is located on Boulevard St Germain) is located in a diverse, multicultural and lively neighbourhood and is housed in the converted premises of a former Turkish bath. The store is small and minimal but with colourful accents. It changes from day to night, becoming a gallery of video images after dark.

The facade is glass but with a ghostly fogging effect, and the Pleats Please signage folds in and out like a pleat. The interior space is dominated by two installations. The first of these 'retail sculptures' is a vivid honeycomb, made out of aluminium, which serves as both a display case and a storage unit. The second is a cool blue cube, made from enamelled steel, which contains the sales counter and gives access to the fitting rooms. This deep azure shade penetrates the room and is a refreshing touch to the otherwise brick and stone of Parisian streets. The result of the interior design gives this small tight space an airy and spacious ambience.

In contrast, the Pleats Please store in Aoyama, Tokyo, boasts an interior full of natural light. It is stark and, apart from a striking curtain made from neoprene that covers one wall of the shop, the only sources of colour are from Issey Miyake's fantastic garments. (The curtain's colour changes according to season.)

The store has silver-grey flooring on the ground level and a silvery-grey ceiling on the first floor, encapsulating the entire space in a silvery shell. Transparent tables and stools in varying heights, made from stainless steel and acrylic, act as display units for accessories, leaving all emphasis to be placed on Miyake's designs. On entering the store the client is confronted with the stairs to the upper floor or a 'bridge' to another section – designed to give clients views of garments from different angles and encourage them to explore.

Above: **Pleats Please Paris.** The facade is glass but with a ghostly fogging effect with the Pleats Please signage folding in and out like a pleat. Miyake's designs stand out even from the street as the only colour and distinct objects in view

Right: **Pleats Please Paris.** The honeycomb installation, made from aluminium, acts as both display case and storage unit. An amusing and innovative solution for retail display

Above left and right: **Pleats Please Paris.** Views of the cool blue cube. Fitting rooms are also accessed from this area, as well as the concealed counter. This use of 360 degrees of blue gives the otherwise small store a feeling of spaciousness

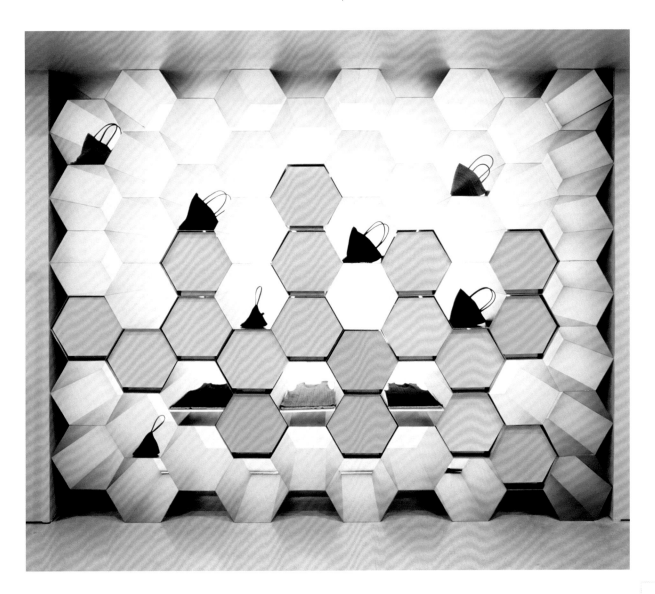

Left, top and bottom: **Pleats Please Tokyo.** Night view of the two-storey building from the street. The vibrant-coloured neoprene curtain gives some sense of scale to the store whilst the garments offer the only other source of colour

Right: **Pleats Please Tokyo.** Garments and accessories compose the space with their distinct colours, like sculptures in a translucent and steel-edged room

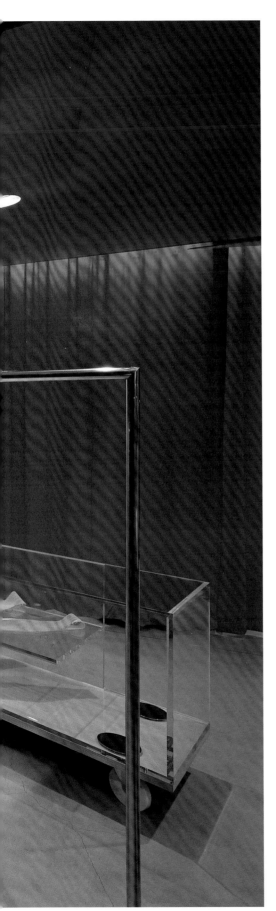

Left: **Pleats Please Tokyo**. The first floor continues with the theme of the curtain and directs all attention to the garments, which are sparsely hung on the minimal stainless-steel rails

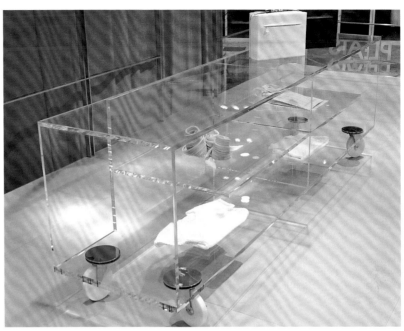

Above: **Pleats Please Tokyo.** Detail of the transparent acrylic accessory tables on wheels. The table is almost invisible suggesting that the accessories are floating in the store

Below: **Pleats Please Tokyo.**
Detail of standing tables and stools made from steel

Cho Slade Architecture
with GaA Architects

Martine Sitbon

Seoul 2002

Commissioned to provide a Seoul home for the fashions of French designer Martine Sitbon, Cho Slade of New York, with local architects GaA Architects, crafted a jewellery box out of a former townhouse in the Cheongdam-dong shopping district. Both classic and modern, the fashions of Martine Sitbon change from season to season, a characteristic that the architects considered when designing the 'timeless' space that would host the collections. The half-buried commercial area at the base of the house was originally the garage and storage areas, with ceiling heights ranging from 1.75 metres to 6 metres. Cho Slade exploited this restrictive characteristic of the building by wrapping the entire interior volume in a continuous surface that bends around corners, floors and ceiling.

The exterior is a glass skin made up of two rows 12.5 metres wide by 3.6 metres tall, stacked on top of one another to create a glass wall at the end of the building. During the day the top row of glass reflects the blue of the sky, while the ground floor row offers a transparent view into the store. At night, the building transforms into a mirrored wall that, rather than reflecting the surrounding neighbourhood, reveals the strong solidity of a wall with its rough polyester paint.

Clothes are displayed using objects in the space: suspended, they appear to float or are subject to the tensions of the architectural dynamics that seamlessly connect the varying heights of the ceiling. The weightlessness is enhanced by the backdrop of a uniform surface compound that literally wraps the floor, walls and ceiling. Whilst glass is the store's outer skin, a buttery-yellow glistening skin envelopes the interior. This glossy finish could give a 'flashy' feel to the store, but is played down due to its neutral tone and the contemporary nature of the display.

The verticality of the movable display racks exaggerates the tightness of the space. The warped surface of the front side of the racks implies a liquid shaped by surface tension, while the mirrored backs, together with the glass shelf and dressing-room mirror, provide a sharp-edged counterpoint to the rounded edges of the space.

The sales counter is made of soft silicone whose smooth edges welcome both client and salesperson. The finish looks much the same as the walls and floor, but in contrast is soft and squishy.

Above **Martine Sitbon Seoul.** The far end of the glass facade offers a preview of the store as well as reflecting the neighbourhood's urban fabric

Above and right: **Martine Sitbon Seoul.** Day through to dusk, the store's glass skin changes to accommodate the differing reflections of each time of day – from blue sky to the towers of adjacent buildings

Left: Martine Sitbon Seoul. The buttery interior skin, with its changing ceiling, offers a smooth and silky backdrop to the sharp-edge of the hanging units

Left: Martine Sitbon Seoul. The shiny low black display object is like an oversized polished pebble. It reveals the height and width of the space in its rounded reflections

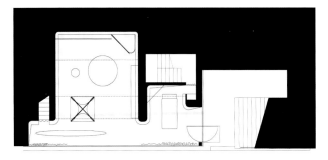

Above: **Martine Sitbon Seoul.** Plan

Below: **Martine Sitbon Seoul.** A wide view of the interior of the store, with the black polished oversized pebble dominating the floor space

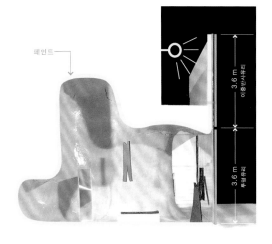

페인트

3.6 m 이중반사유리

3.6 m 투영유리

Above: **Martine Sitbon Seoul.** Section

Above: **Martine Sitbon Seoul.** Garments are suspended and float in the space, whilst interrupted by the sharp edges of the mirrored screen. The cocoon-like linear object that floats behind the facade accentuates the length of the space and the symmetry between floor and ceiling

Above: **Martine Sitbon Seoul.** Daytime view of the entrance and facade

Above: **Martine Sitbon Seoul.** The store at night almost glows, with a rusted golden hue to the upper floor

Right: **Martine Sitbon Seoul.** The length of the transparent facade at night, with the soft silicone cash desk between two dressed mannequins in the foreground

6a Architects
with Tom Emerson

Oki-ni

London 2001

The distinctive architectural treatment of Oki-ni expresses a departure from a usual retail concept – it's a 'shopfront' for clothes that are only available online from the Oki-ni website. So why have a store if the actual act of the sale happens in cyberspace and not real space?

Oki-ni is offering the fashion market a new relationship between client and product: limited edition clothes and accessories by well-known brands, such as Oki-ni/Adidas Handball Spezial trainers, are available only via the internet from Oki-ni. However, fashion is a tactile business, and the total experience of the 'shop' has always been more than just a point of sale.

6a Architects won the commission to design this store (and the concessions that followed) with an installation-based concept that emphasises the tactile and social opportunities of clothes in the shopping environment. The three large windows which make up its facade reveal a felt landscape contained by an oak 'tray' inserted into the existing concrete shell. The steep upward sides of the fan-shaped tray divide the main shop from the changing room but primarily serve as an oddly domestic hanging rail for clothes. The walls that are visible above the tray's sides are made of rough, unfinished concrete that provides a contrast of textures.

There is no traditional shelving. Apart from on the tray walls, the other displays are laid out on top of large, rectangular piles of felt, which can also be used as furniture, and hollow metal lengths. The hollows provide space for a low level library of books about design, art and photography.

With all transactions conducted online, the point of sale is missing, and so too are the cash desks. 6a have avoided any obvious concentration of technology and a laptop provides the sales interface. This is meant to be casually placed amongst the products and visitors, but in truth, it is usually set in front of a shop assistant, standing at what could be mistaken for a lectern. 6a Architects has won major awards for the design of Oki-ni, but are we ready for it? The assistants have to explain the concept to first-time shoppers, while it seems unlikely that many people really are going to make room amongst the diplays so they can lounge about and read a book.

It is interesting that the London store is situated on Savile Row, a street famous the world over for traditional men's tailoring. With its limited editions, Oki-ni is leaning towards a bespoke service and its heavy use of wood can be seen as derivative of the conventional wood panelling of establishment tailors. Its position at the north end of the street also places it within the immediate vicinity of the design, new media and film companies whose employees are most likely to feel at home in this retail adventure.

Above: Oki-ni London. The store, seen from Savile Row, has three large windows that give it a very expansive, open image

Right and below: **Oki-ni London.** The large piles of felt act as both display units and furniture. Explicit lighting, using low hung bare bulbs, gives the store its studio feel

Above: Oki-ni London. Clothes hang from the low sides of the oak tray in a casual domestic way, as though in one's own bedroom

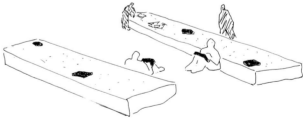

Above: Oki-ni London. Concept sketch of customers using the felt piles as furniture and lay out tables

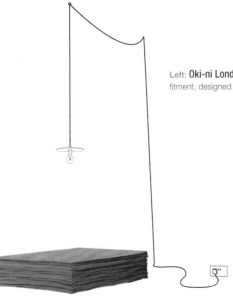

Left: Oki-ni London. Drawing of light-bulb fitment, designed by 6A, above felt piles

Above: Oki-ni London. Model of the oak tray that has been inserted into the store space

Above: **Oki-ni London.** The laptop is the only reference to technology in the store, and acts as a sales interface, but not the sale itself. It is casually placed on the felt pile for both clients and store assistants to use

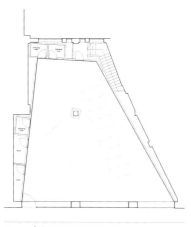

Above: **Oki-ni London.** Plan of store

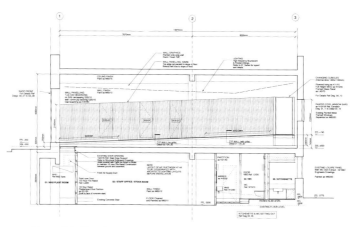

Above: **Oki-ni London.** Section of store

Gabellini Associates
with Gianfranco Ferré

Gianfranco Ferré Boutique

Milan 2003

Gianfranco Ferré's fashion designs are known for their weight – in luxury, in presence, in fabrics, in design. It is an international name but very much rooted in Italy. Gianfranco Ferré himself first trained as an architect before turning his talents to fashion design, and now produces strong lines for both mens and womens- wear. Seen as a collaboration, Gabellini Associates (based in New York), initiated the basic architectural concepts for this prominent store in the heart of Milan, and Gianfranco Ferré's architectural talents completed the details and gave it its finishing touches.

Not only is this boutique remarkable in its real estate – the store spans across an archway on the second floor of this period building, that leads to a zen-like courtyard – but the first of its kind to also house a Spa. Shopping and Spa's have finally found each other! It is not obvious what the connections are between high-fashion and Spa's, other than both are luxurious, but the dominating factor behind this combination is due to the fact that they are both owned by the same parent company (IT Holdings). The Spa is, in this case, absolutely luxurious and despite being in a tight urban setting, looks out onto the green and pebbled courtyard at the back of the building.

The store itself is spread across two levels and lies symmetrically either side of the front-entrance archway, with menswear to the left and womenswear to the right (with a hallway linking the store from womenswear to the Ferré Spa). The various spaces are defined by distinct interior elements and connected through the continuity of textures, shapes and lines. The use of folding panels and mobile screens in addition, give each space its own flexibility.

The spaces are luxurious and no expense has been spared in choice of materials and attention to detail. The backdrop is dominated by red, mostly in panels, giving the store its intimate and sensuous edge, and the abundant use of dark woods adds to this deep-coloured environment. Accessory cases are made from rare woods – zebrano and mahogany – and given a gloss-finish to show off its superb grain. Sofas are made from precious leathers and trays from mother-of-pearl mosaics. Wallcovers for the mens area tends to be leather panelling, whilst silk for the womens area. In contrast, beige and red tones are found dotted throughout the store and a soft pink hue sets the ground-floor womens section unmistakably apart from the rest.

Above: **Gianfranco Ferré, Milan.** The stairway, in red resin glass with carpeted steel chrome steps, leads up to the first floor to the womenswear.

Above: **Gianfranco Ferré, Milan.** Mica screens and luxurious accessory cabinets. Precious leather pouches and open-trunks housing other accessories in the background.

Above, below and right: **Gianfranco Ferré, Milan**. View through to mensewar at the back of the store, that overlooks the courtyard. The back section is wall panelled in red leather.

Gabellini Associates

Nicole Farhi

New York 1999

The Nicole Farhi store in New York is a prime example of where fashion retail has extended beyond itself into other areas of business which, hopefully, still enhance the brand. In this case, fashion merges with fine dining and the brand has also lent itself to a homeware range. Whilst still very much a store dedicated to Nicole Farhi's collection of elegant fashions in typically refined textiles, the 1999 venture was significant in pushing the boundaries of what fashion symbolises today. Michael Gabellini, known for his minimalist interior architecture that utilises touches of sensuality, was the perfect match for Farhi.

The New York store occupies a 1901 landmark building which was formerly home to the famous Copacabana nightclub. The exterior of the Beaux Arts building was restored with Indiana limestone and Deer Isle granite in order to complement the original stone. The entrance to the store brings the customer across a glass bridge which runs between two double height atria and leads into womenswear, which effectively hovers over the basement restaurant. This 'floating platform' is comprised of American walnut and honed New York bluestone floors. The latter visually connects the floor to the blue-plaster ceiling of the restaurant below.

Two staircases lead down from womenswear, one directly into the restaurant and the other to the home and menswear collections. From this level, there is another entrance to the restaurant via floating wooden steps. The overall effect of the bridge and atria is to give due prominence to the restaurant, even though it is in the lower level. 4,000 square feet, over one third of the retail space, is given over to the dining area which has significant architectural features, including a 30-foot-long luminescent bar-table and a seemingly floating glass cube that houses the open kitchen.

Farhi was far better known in London than New York when she opened this two-pronged venture, but this retail and restaurant synthesis has proven to be successful.

Above: **Nicole Farhi New York.** The 1901 landmark building at night

Right: **Nicole Farhi New York.** The 4,000-square-foot restaurant is marked by a 30-foot-long luminescent bar-table, but the main focus is the water-white glass cube floating on a raised bluestone plinth that houses the open kitchen

New Departments

Department stores have always offered interior architects a wide scope for display design. Ever since their conception, the work of interior architects has vied to attract customers with displays of anything from the exotic to the traditional, side by side, and under one huge roof. This competition for attention still dominates the collage of floors today. As the customer passes from fragrance to cosmetics, neckties to handbags, and wine to cheese, numerous forms of installations are crying out for custom. Department stores are busy places, not just in terms of customer traffic, but in terms of visual display.

Traditionally, they have been housed in grand architecture that reflected the times of the international expositions – when countries were competing in terms of their international grasp of the world in the late 19th and early 20th centuries. In both the Gallerie Lafayette in Paris and the Galleria Vittorio Emanuele in Milan, the decorative, stained-glass, overarching roofs represented the height of decadence and luxury.

In the early 21st century, it seems that some department stores are relooking at the shell that houses them and are seeking to put themselves back on the fashionable retail map by commissioning signature architects to

New Departments

redesign them. Presently, this seems to be a phenomena limited to the UK, though this is not to say that the department stores of the US, France and Germany are ignoring their interior architectural content. Rather, to date there have been no other examples of serious investments in new, innovative architecture for department stores other than in the UK. And the prime example is Selfridges.

Selfridges was founded in 1909 with the opening of its Oxford Street store and marked a new era in retailing. It was the largest building to be designed as a single store and, with over 500,000 square feet of trading floor, it is still the biggest store on London's Oxford Street. It was the first store to introduce the modern window display and to put perfumery at the front of the store to lure shoppers in from the street – aspects of department stores that are now taken for granted.

Nearly one hundred years on, Selfridges 2003 is marking another turning point in department store history. By inviting contemporary architects Future Systems to give them a new architectural image, Selfridges have broken new ground for both retail and architecture.

Selfridges Birmingham, its fourth UK store, was to establish an iconic building not just for Selfridges but also for the city. The building, inspired by a Paco Rabanne dress, is clad with 16,000 aluminium discs on a blue wave, giving the Birmingham skyline an incredible interruption from its typical roofscapes and buildings. Within weeks of its opening, the building was adopted by the city as its landmark. Moreover, the incredible, futuristically styled facade had attacted the attention of the international press – and all in the name of a department store. Despite having no signage on the exterior, it seems the whole world knows whose store this is.

Selfridges has also put serious investment into the interiors of its stores. Although the work can be seen as a 'squeeze' of styles in an almost cramped space, the concessions for the big brands have carried their signature architects with them under the umbrella of designers like Stanton Williams and Future Systems for the overall concepts. The cities of Manchester and Birmingham have been particularly receptive to this restyling as the cities themselves experience a change to their overall architectural and cultural landscape. Seen as style-conscious, thriving urban centres, offering an alternative to London, both Selfridges and Harvey Nichols have put their names firmly on the city maps.

Vittorio Radice, the man who was the energy behind this new approach to architecture for Selfridges and who led the Birmingham store into being, is now leading Marks and Spencer into new design territory. Though a brand in its own right and firmly entrenched on almost every UK high street, Marks and Spencer has enjoyed a very conservative image to date. However, disappointing recent figures have prompted reconsideration of this image and in response their new 'lifestyle' stores are experimenting with design and architecture. Radice has commissioned minimalist guru John Pawson to design the first of the Lifestores in Gateshead, near Newcastle, to carry the message.

Radice has clearly been an influential figure in bringing new architecture and design to the world of department stores, believing that customers really do 'buy into' the idea of lifestyle when shopping for garments or objects. Commissioning Pawson for the new lifestyle store and design guru Tyler Brûlé (former founder of *Wallpaper**) to design the new catalogue for the store, Marks and Spencer may finally shake off its 'safe' image. We shall wait and see.

Stanton Williams

Selfridges

Manchester 2002

Above: **Selfridges Manchester.** The new five-storey Selfridges is located right in Manchester's city centre on Exchange Square, designed by Tadao Ando

Selfridges' first venture outside London, part of the 1998 Trafford Centre in south Manchester, was commercially significant but of little interest architecturally. However, the move reflected the cultural and retail regeneration of the city: top brands were selling to a somewhat untapped mass of style-conscious, cultural urbanites with surplus income. It seems no coincidence that this burgeoning of a fashion-savvy populace happened at the same time as the huge architectural renaissance of the city (which was partly spurred on by the devastation caused by the IRA bomb of 1996).

The Lowry Centre, the Imperial War Museum, the rebuilt Royal Exchange and the defining of Canal Street as an ultra-cool gay area were all instrumental in placing Manchester at the forefront of national culture. Mancunians just needed the clothes and accessories to match. Encouraged by the success of the Trafford branch, Vittorio Radice took Selfridges into the heart of the city in 2002 with a second store that clearly outlined the company's intent to be at the centre of the UK's urban renewal.

Marks & Spencer's own new store in the Trafford Centre had found its 31,000 square metre central Manchester outlet short of customers, so it chose to halve its space and create room for a new Selfridges with a prime facade on Tadao Ando's new Exchange Square. The sheer glass curtain of the facade has a great functional use as a display area for huge posters highlighting this season's look, but the real story is inside, where the concept of the department store took a leap forward.

Stanton Williams was given the brief to co-ordinate the redesign, which

Above and left: **Selfridges Manchester.** David Adjaye has used glass and mirrors to help create a welcoming, airy space on the ground floor. Humorous touches include the sunglasses display case in the shape of a huge eye

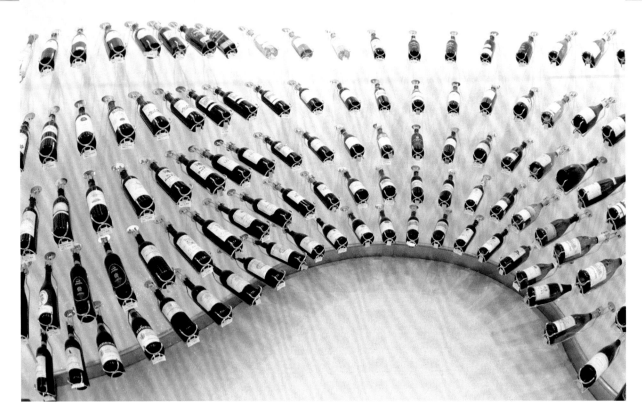

Above: **Selfridges Manchester.** Future Systems' curvaceous wine rack in the food hall hints at the practice's future design for the exterior of Selfridges Birmingham

involves a central interior street dividing Selfridges from the reduced M&S, but each of the five floors was designed by a different high-profile practice, thereby encouraging the image of Selfridges as an innovative leader in many diverse 'departments'. David Adjaye, the London maestro of contemporary chic, designed the all-important ground floor space for beauty and accessories. His undulating ceiling and sensitive use of glass coax the shopper into the heart of the store, while visual jokes remind them that they are supposed to be having fun. Future Systems, known for its ability to bring curves to the most unlikely of places, took on the food hall, creating an explosion of curved cabinets surrounded by a wall of waves.

Stanton Williams itself designed womenswear on the second floor, and also the impressive cantilevered restaurant on the top floor, which breaks through the inner facade to be suspended above the interior street. The menswear floor, typified by masculine solidity of both form and colour, is designed by Belgian architect Vincent Van Duysen, while Cibic and Partners created identifiable areas for the multipurpose fourth floor.

Selfridges had gone beyond both its geographical limitations and the supposed constraints of interior architecture for department stores. The next step was to combine its multi-architect approach to interiors with a landmark exterior for another large, regional centre – Birmingham.

Above: **Selfridges Manchester.** Mannequins are suspended just above the floor in Stanton Williams' design for the womenswear floor. The striped ceiling and palette of clean, pale materials help orientate the shopper and emphasise the displays

Future Systems

Selfridges

Birmingham 2003

Like Manchester, Birmingham has undergone a massive central redevelopment in recent years, which has included a new canalside cultural quarter, a greater focus on the arts and the introduction of upmarket retail ventures such as the Mailbox. With the success of Selfridges Manchester, Vittorio Radice decided to continue the department store's expansion beyond its famous central London Oxford Street store with an architectural landmark for the UK's second largest city.

This was a bold stroke and required a bold architectural partner: Future Systems, who also worked with Radice on radical designs for the Manchester branch's food hall. Its design for the exterior of the Birmingham store was to be another leap forward. Stemming from a Paco Rabanne dress and other more organic natural forms, the result was a departure from any other department store to date. Selfridges Birmingham opened in September 2003 and has been a huge success for Selfridges, Future Systems and Birmigham itself.

Situated in Birmingham's 'Bull Ring', the site offered a pretty mixed backdrop of red brick, modern retail and grey ringroads. The Bull Ring is the site of the traditional marketplace and this has been continued in its new development in the form of a mixed retail and shopping mall. Directly opposite the site is St Martin's Church, a Victorian neo-Gothic church that is perhaps the only historic building in the site's immedite vicinity.

Working within this context, Future Systems' architecture provides a strikingly alternative backdrop for St Martin's angular and vertical neo-Gothic style. The building's form makes reference to the fall of fabric, and its skin curves around the inner shell like the soft lines of a body; there is no distinction between walls and roof, and no angles that break this organic flow of fabric. It is one continuous movement of architecture and interrupts the city's environment with its horizon of a scaly blue wave.

Inspired by the sequins on the 1960s Paco Rabanne dress, and the movement of the 'chain-dress', also by Paco Rabanne, the exterior of the building is enveloped in a skin made up of 16,000 aluminium discs, creating a lustrous grain. The pattern is constant, like that of a fly's eye, and follows the rhythms of the curves as discs are placed slightly closer together or further apart. In bright sunlight, the discs shimmer, and similarly reflect the changing weather conditions. Combined with its aluminium wave of a 'skirting board' that lines the bottom of the building, the building takes on the colours and shapes of the people or things that pass by. It creates a most distinct surface area that literally glows amongst the skyline of its

Above: **Selfridges Birmingham.** The wave (right) was inspired by the sequins on the 1960s Paco Rabanne dress (top), and the movement of the 'chain-dress' (above) also by Paco Rabanne. The exterior of the building is enveloped in a skin made up of 16,000 aluminium discs, creating a lustrous grain

neighbouring buildings. The surface onto which the discs are attached is painted a deep 'Yves Klein' blue, and is flooded with blue light at night – allowing the discs to sit in shadow and the blue background to glow.

The lid of the building has a free-form opening that pours down light into a great atrium, permitting a clear view of the sky from within and giving a very real sense of the weather conditions outside. Large, sinuously shaped openings carved from the form offer themselves as display windows and are the only view out of the store other than the upward reaching skylight.

The four-storey building has four entrances on three different levels: one of which is from a spectacular 17-metre-high pedestrian bridge leading from the multistorey car park.

The key to Future Systems' interior is the deep atrium, criss-crossed by a white-clad cat's cradle of escalators that holds the floors together, whilst also setting up a play on textures – the handrails are made from glossy fibreglass, while the undersides of the escalators are clad in matt plaster.

As with the Manchester store, different designers were commissioned to create the interior, resulting in four very distinct retail areas. Future Systems designed Level 1 which includes the food hall and other levels were designed by Eldridge Williams, Stanton Williams and Cibic Partners/Lees Associates.

Below: **Selfridges Birmingham.** Twilight. The outstanding building creates the most distinct surface area that literally glows amongst the skyline of its neighbouring structures

Above: **Selfridges Birmingham.** The four-storey building has four entrances on three different levels, one of which is from a spectacular 17-metre-high pedestrian bridge leading from the multistorey car park

Above and right: **Selfridges Birmingham.** The interior of the building is a deep atrium, criss-crossed by a white-clad 'cat's cradle' of escalators that holds the floors together

Above: **Selfridges Birmingham.** The surface to which the discs are attached is painted a deep 'Yves Klein' blue, and is flooded with blue light at night – allowing the discs to sit in shadow and the blue background to glow

Selfridges Birmingham. Cut away

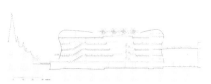

Selfridges Birmingham. Section

Selfridges Birmingham. Site plan

Four IV

Harvey Nichols
Manchester 2003

Above: **Harvey Nichols Edinburgh.** Exterior of the Harvey Nichols' store in Edinburgh. Its interior design led the way for the Manchester branch

Harvey Nichols, a major focal point for Knightsbridge chic and 'ladies who lunch', first ventured north when its Leeds store opened in 1996. This was followed by a 2002 opening in Edinburgh which was so successful that it was forced to shut its doors within hours of opening due to the crush. It is this Edinburgh store, with an interior by Four IV and a restaurant designed by Lifschutz Davidson, that paved the way for the interior look of the 2003 Manchester branch.

With its Leeds venture, Harvey Nichols was acting on the same realisation that had initiated the expansion of Selfridges. The cultural regeneration of certain British cities, marked by an investment in new architecture and stylish new bars and restaurants, was underway and there was a readymade youthful, market who no longer wanted to look towards London for entertainment and style. It was only a question of time before Harvey Nichols set up shop near Manchester's Exchange Square, right next door to Selfridges.

Masterplanned by Building Design Partnership, the building is a stone clad pavilion (which is typical of Manchester's retail architecture) with a double-height glass frontage for the entranceway. Its major distinctive feature is a glass tower on the corner which displays the Harvey Nichols' logo and can be illuminated at night.

Inside, Four IV has gone for subtlety, with pale colours and tinted glass, but has used a golden staircase to guide the customer from the cosmetics section to accessories. Womenswear is dressed with tall lampstands and pink drapes, while a feeling of light and space is aided by a limestone floor and a very linear display arrangement. The restaurant and bar areas are of huge importance to the image of Harvey Nichols. The red, pin-cushion frontage of the bar, the curving seats of the bar stools and the polished, black granite floor give a sense of style to rival that of the London flagship. The restaurant has the bonus of overlooking Tadao Ando's Exchange Square, the new cultural heart of the city.

Harvey Nichols may not be intending to roll out any more British standalone stores, but its investment in cities outside London has paved the way for the company's future:

It is now looking abroad to expand but chief executive Joseph Wan is interested in India, Turkey and South America rather than Paris and New York, saying, 'They each have high populations with rapidly growing proportions of wealthy customers.'

Above: **Harvey Nichols Manchester.** The Manchester exterior and glass tower, seen from Tadao Ando's Exchange Square, which has become the central feature of Manchester's regeneration

Below: **Harvey Nichols Manchester.** The bar, with its polished marble floor and pin cushion frontage, is a prime destination for cocktail-drinkers

Above: **Harvey Nichols Manchester.** Four IV have gone for light materials and very clear routes in womenswear, adding subtle touches of pink

John Pawson

Marks & Spencer Lifestore
Gateshead 2004

Above: **Marks & Spencer Lifestore Gateshead.** Exterior of John Pawson's minimalist two-storey house, built within the store

Marks & Spencer's creation of Lifestores, a new chain focusing on furniture and homeware, is more about 'lifestyle' than fashion retail but it is still very interesting due to the involvement of Vittorio Radice, who led the northwards expansion of Selfridges and restored the fortunes of Habitat. This move is a bold attempt to bring a new 'style' concept to the mid-market masses whilst changing the safe image of the high street giant, M&S.

The first Lifestore opens in Gateshead just as this book is going to press. The location is no surprise as the town's sensational renaissance as a cultural destination, due to Anthony Gormley's 'Angel of the North' and the 'winking eye' bridge, has made it ripe for this venture in the same way as Manchester and Birmingham were perfect for Selfridges. In an interview with *Icon* (September 2003) Radice described the decision as 'just lucky', but what is certainly beyond luck is the involvement of John Pawson.

John Pawson ensured that fashion became an obedient recipient of his ideas when he designed Calvin Klein's Manhattan store in 1995. His ultra-minimalist style, featuring distilled neo-classical lines and huge single panes of glass, set the tone for fashion retail for the rest of the 20th century. In truth, he has designed very few fashion stores outside his work for Calvin Klein: his real obsession is with the 'living space', displayed through his design of private houses, showrooms for domestic interiors, and household objects. In 2001, he even co-wrote a cookery book, *Living and Eating*, which explored the concept of home dining within simple, minimalist interiors. In short, Radice had lined up the perfect partner for the new M&S vision.

The Gateshead store is just a white shed, or a 'factory' as Radice calls it, on the outskirts of town. Inside, Pawson has designed the simplest of interiors to provide a pure backdrop to an eclectic range of goods and colours which are arranged in nine lifestyle zones such as 'relax' and 'renew'. This mix of utilitarianism and 'high concept shopping' could lead to criticism but, in the end, the customer will be the judge. What does seem more extraordinarily refreshing is that Pawson has built a lifesize, two-storey display house within the store. Classically Pawsonesque, with long stretches of glass, a cedar clad and white concrete exterior, and a light interior featuring pale flooring and the more minimalist of M&S's furnishings, the house has exterior and interior staircases for ease of public access. It is planned that a different architect will build a new interior house every year.

Lifestore is augmented by a new lifestyle catalogue designed by Tyler Brûlé, the founder of the successful style magazine *Wallpaper**. Radice has made a serious statement of intent that will, in one way or another, change our relationship with Marks & Spencer forever.

Right: **Marks & Spencer Lifestore Gateshead.** The bathroom of the house, featuring minimalist fixtures and stone fittings including a stone, rectangular washbasin

Listings – Store Details

Alexander McQueen
www.alexandermcqueen.net

Via Verri 8
Milan 20121
Italy
Tel +39 02 76 003374

4–5 Old Bond Street
London W1S 4PD
UK
Tel +44 (0)20 7355 0088

417 West 14th Street
New York
NY 10014
USA
Tel +1 212 645 1797

Burberry
www.burberry.com

Via Verri 7
Milan 20121
Italy
Tel +39 02 76 08201

Chloe
www.chloe.com

152–3 Sloane Street
London SW1X 9BX
UK
Tel +44 (0)20 782 35348

Comme des Garçons

16 Place Vendôme
Paris 75001
France
Tel +33 (0)147 036090

5–2–1 Minamiaoyama
Minato-ku
Tokyo 107
Japan
Tel + 81 (0)3 406 3951

116 Wooster Street
New York
NY 10012
USA
Tel +1 212 219 0660

Dolce & Gabbana
www.dolcegabbana.it

6–8 Old Bond Street
London W1S 4PJ
UK
Tel +44 (0)20 7659 9000

825 Madison Avenue
New York NY 10021
USA
Tel +1 212 2494100

Emporio Armani
www.emporioarmani.com

Emporio Armani/Chater
House
11 Chater Road
Central
Hong Kong SAR
Tel +852 (0)2532 7711
Fax +852 (0)2532 7719

601 Madison Avenue
New York NY 10022
USA
Tel +1 212 317 0800
Fax +1 212 317 8616

410 West Broadway
New York NY 10012
USA
Tel +1 646 613 8099
Fax +1 646 613 8292

Fendi
www.fendi.com

24 Rue François 1er
Paris 7500
France
Tel +33 (0)149 528452
Fax +33 (0)149 529868

Via Borgognona 36–40
Rome 00187
Italy
Tel +39 06 696661
Fax +39 06 69940808

20–2 Sloane Street
London SW1X 9NE
UK
Tel +44 (0)20 7838 6288
Tel +44 (0)20 7838 6289

Gianfranco Ferré
www.gianfrancoferre.com

Via Sant'Andrea 15
Milan 20121
Italy
Tel +39 02 79 48 64

Giorgio Armani
www.giorgioarmani.com

2093 Rua Bela Cinta
Cerquiera Cesar
São Paulo 01415–002
Brazil
Tel +55 (0)11 3062 2660
Fax +55 (0)11 3897 9071

6 Place Vendôme
Paris 75001
France
Tel +33 (0)142 615509
Fax +33 (0)140 150731

Via Sant'Andrea 9
Milan 20121
Italy
Tel +39 02 76 003234
Fax +39 02 76 014926

37 Sloane Street
London SW1X 9LP
UK
Tel +44 (0)20 7235 6232
Fax +44 (0)20 7823 1342

Harvey Nichols
www.harveynichols.com

21 New Cathedral Street
Manchester M1 1AD
UK
Tel +44 (0)161 828 8888
Fax +44 (0)161 828 8833

Hermès
www.hermes.com

4-1 Ginza 5-chome
Chuo-ku
Tokyo 104–0061
Japan
Tel +81 (0)3 3289 6811
Fax +81 (0)3 3289 6812

Jil Sander
www.jilsander.com

32-4 Osterfeldstrasse
Hamburg 22529
Germany
Tel +49 (0)40 553 02 0
Fax +49 (0)40 553 30 34

7 Burlington Gardens
London W1S 3ES
UK
Tel +44 (0)20 7758 1000

11 East 57th Street
New York
NY 10022
USA
Tel +1 212 8386100

Louis Vuitton
www.vuitton.com

22 Avenue Montaigne
Paris 75008
France
Tel +33 (0)810 810 010

Nagoya Sakae
3–16–17 Nishiki
Naka-ku
Nagoya 460-0003
Japan
Tel +81 (0)5 2957 3051

3–6–1 Ginza Chuo-Ku
Tokyo 104-8130
Japan
Tel +81 (0)3 3567 1211

Roppongi Keyakizaka Dori
Roppongi Hills
6–12–3 Roppongi Minato-ku
Tokyo 106-0032
Japan
Tel +81 (0)3 3478 2100

5–7–5 Jingumae Shibuya-ku
Omotesando
Tokyo 150-0001
Japan
Tel +81 (0)3 3478 2211

99–18 Chungdam-Dong
Kangnam-Ku
Seoul 135-100
South Korea
Tel +82 (0)2 548 21 65
Fax +82 (0)2 548 21 62

116 Greene Street
New York NY 10012
USA
Tel +1 212 274 9090
Fax +1 212 274 8789

Marks & Spencer Lifestore
www.marksandspencer.com

Metro Park North
Gibside Way
Gateshead NE11 9BT
UK
Tel +44 (0)191 401 1200

Marni
www.marni.it

57 Avenue Montaigne
Paris 75008
France
Tel +33 (0)156 880808

Via Sismondi 70
Milan 20133
Italy
Tel +39 02 70 005479
Fax +39 02 71 040309

26 Sloane Street
London SW1X 9NE
UK
Tel +44 (0)20 7245 9520

161 Mercer St.
New York NY 10012
USA
Tel +1 212 343 3912

Martine Sitbon
89–20 Chungdam-Dong
Kangnam–ku
Seoul 135–100
South Korea
Tel + 82 2 542 0095

Nicole Farhi
www.nicolefarhi.com

10 East 60th Street
New York NY 10022
USA
Tel +1 212 223 8811

Oki-ni
www.okini.com

25 Savile Row
London W1S 3PR
UK
Tel +44 (0)207 494 1716

Paul Smith
www.paulsmith.co.uk

Palazzo Gallarati Scotti
Via Manzoni 30
Milan 20121
Italy
Tel +39 02 76 319181

Westbourne House
122 Kensington Park Road
London W11 2EP
UK
Tel +44 (0)20 7727 3553

Pleats Please
www.pleatsplease.com

3 rue des Rosiers
Paris 75004
France
Tel +33 (0)140 299966

La Place de Minami Aoyama
3–13–21 Minami-Aoyama
Minato-ku
Tokyo 107-0062
Japan
Tel +81 (0)3 5772 7750

Prada
www.prada.com

5–2–6 Minami-Aoyama
Minato-ku
Tokyo 107-0062
Japan
Tel +81 (0)3 6418 0400

575 Broadway
New York NY 10012
USA
Tel +1 212 334-8888

Selfridges
www.selfridges.com

Upper Mall East
Bull Ring
Birmingham B5 4BP
UK
Tel +44 (0)8708 377377

1 Exchange Square
Manchester M3 1BD
UK
Tel +44 (0)8708 377377

Stella McCartney
www.stellamccartney.com

30 Bruton Street
London W1J 6LG
UK
Tel +44 (0)20 7518 3100

429 West 14th Street
New York NY 10014
USA
Tel +1 212 255 1556

Bibliography

Publications

Antonello Boschi (editor), *Showrooms*, teNeues (Kempen), 2001

Helen Castle (editor), *Architectural Design - Fashion + Architecture*, Vol 70, No 6, Wiley-Academy, 2000

Deborah Fausch, Paulette Singley, Rodolphe El-Khourj, Zvi Efrah (editors), *Architecture: In Fashion*, Princeton Architectural Press (New York), 1994

Inclusive: The Architecture of Louis Vuitton, 2003 (to accompany the exhibition 'Inclusive: 1 Brand, 6 Architects, 11 Projects', Berlin 2003), AedesBerlin (Berlin), 2003

Logique/Visuelle: The Architecture of Louis Vuitton 2003 (to accompany the exhibition 'Mathematique des Objets Sensibles' held at LV Hall and Tokyo International Forum April 2003), Louis Vuitton (Japan), 2003

Otto Riewoldt, *Retail Design*, Laurence King (London), 2000

Articles

Susie Boyt, 'Where You'll Shop Next', *Financial Times Weekend*, 31 August 2003, p W4

Grace Bradbury, 'The Gospel According to Paul Smith', *Evening Standard Magazine*, 13 February 2004, pp 26-9

'The Case for Brands', *The Economist*, 6 September 2001, seen at www.economist.com

'A Costly Luxury', *The Economist*, 6 February 2003, seen at www.economist.com

Ed Crooks and Susanna Voyke, 'Comment & Analysis: The mindset is one we haven't seen for quite a while: people are worried, there's a real reluctance to spend', *Financial Times*, 28 June 2003, seen at www.ft.com

'Don't Mix your Designers', *The Economist,* 14 January 1999, seen at www.economist.com

'Every Cloud Has a Satin Lining', *The Economist,* 21 March 2002, seen at www.economist.com

Mike Exon, 'New Blood Takes Bland Out of the Brand', *Financial Times – Creative Businesss section*, 10 June 2003, p 6

'Harvey Nichols Opens New Manchester Store', www.manchestercalling.com, 11 August 2003

Edwin Heathcote, 'Architecture: Theatrical Art of High Consumerism', *Financial Times*, 15 September 2003, seen at www.ft.com

Edwin Heathcote, 'Light. Nob. Felt. Things: A Chat with Tom Emerson', in Edwin Heathcote (guest editor), *Architectural Design – Furniture + Architecture*, Vol 72, No 4, 2002, p 72–7

Damian Foxe, 'All About Yves – and Gucci', *Financial Times Weekend*, 20–1 September 2003, p W6

Mark Irving, 'Being Miuccia', *Financial Times Magazine*, 21 June 2003, p 25

'It's shopping but not as we know it', *Marks and Spencer Magazine*, Spring 2004

Craig Kellogg, 'The Matchmaker', in Neil Spiller (guest editor), *Architectural Design – Reflective Architecture*, Vol 72, No 3, 2002, p 98–101

Troy McMullen, 'Louis Vuitton Brands Its Space', *Wall Street Journal*, 13–15 June 2003, p A8

Daniela Mecozzi, 'Selling Style', *Frame*, Vol 30, January-February 2003, seen at www.framemag.com

'Prada Flagship Store, New York', www.galinsky.com

'Radice's Relaxed Vision for Future of M&S', *The Observer*, 25 May 2003, seen at observer/guardian.co.uk

Fiona Rattray, 'Hard Sell', *The Independent*, 27 January 2004, seen at www.independent.co.uk

Paula Reed, 'Daddy Bare', *Observer Food Monthly*, January 2004, p 49–51

'Reinventing the Store', *The Economist – Special Report on Retail,* 22 November 2003, p 89

Stella Shamoon, 'My Gamble with Gucci', *The Mail On Sunday – Financial Mail section*, 1 February 2004, p 7

'When Profits Go Out of Fashion', *The Economist,* 3 July 2003, seen at www.economist.com

Journals

L'Arca, September 2003

Frame, July–August 2003

Architectural Record, September 2003

Harpers & Queen, July 2003

Icon, September 2003

Domus, July–August 2003

Lotus, edition 118, 2003